Praise for *Capability at Work*

"I found the insights in this book had me nodding my head in agreement on almost every page. The practical advice is clear and implementable, so long as the mindsets are primed. I am sure readers will want to keep it close at hand as they help their organisations meet the increasing demands for high performance from their workforces."

Charles Jennings,
Learning and Performance Expert

"Finally, a book which speaks sense. As an L&D professional and experienced lecturer, Paul talks about the things that I have always tried to embed in my teaching and training. That is to develop the ability in the trainee to not just become competent at that moment in time in order to pass an exam or carry out a task, but to become capable in applying and understanding the learning process and being able to apply this to other events and learning in the future to become truly capable through life and career.

Paul's book does what it says on the tin!"

Sue Snowball
Head of Learning and Organisational Development, Coleg Gwent

"*Capability at Work* is in effect a field guide for HR and Learning and Development practitioners to develop performance consulting capability, which is key in providing effective business improvement. Paul Matthews' new book challenges the 'order taking' approach of L&D departments and presents an engaging as well as practical guide for practitioners to develop consulting capabilities."

Karly Olsen-Haveland
Group Director of People and Organisation Development, Impellam Group

"HR and Learning and Development experts have spent years trying to turn their perceived specialism into accepted and essential organisational capabilities. Paul manages to achieve this with simplicity and clarity underpinned by genuine case studies and theory. This book is a must for anyone starting out in the world of HR and L&D as well as for the more seasoned practitioner who has faced the challenges of turning knowledge and competence into capability. A very welcome addition to the business book library"

Colonel Garry Hearn OBE
Defence Learning and Development Transformation Programme

"It is not sufficient to be competent. An L&D department must be capable, and must be able to build the capability of its clients. This book explains why this is so, and lays out practical steps to get you there."

Dave Pearson
Head of R&D IT Learning Service

"This concept is so obvious so why don't we all practice it? L&D professionals need to wake up and smell the coffee, read this and communicate with your stakeholders for great results. A fantastic book Paul."

Tony Bulmer
Learning Design Manager

"Paul Matthews' brilliant new book '*Capability at Work*' is straightforward, practical and effective. An essential guide for all managers to improve individual and organisational performance!"

Meriel Box,
Head of Staff Development

"I always enjoy reading Paul's weekly tips, so am delighted that his latest book brings together his deep insights into learning and development. My big take-away is that training departments should not allow their role to be seen internally as delivering training but as advisers to management."

Richard Chaplin,
Founder & Executive Chairman, Managing Partners' Forum

capability
AT WORK

Paul Matthews

capability
AT WORK

HOW TO SOLVE THE PERFORMANCE PUZZLE

Three Faces Publishing

First published in 2014 by
Three Faces Publishing
Alchemy House
17 Faraday Drive
Milton Keynes
MK5 7DD
United Kingdom

www.threefacespublishing.com
info@threefacespublishing.com

British Library Cataloguing in Publication Data
A CIP catalogue record for this book is available from the British Library

ISBN 978-1-909552-04-3

The Publisher's policy is to use paper manufactured from sustainable forests.

Printed and bound in the UK by TJ International Ltd, Padstow, Cornwall

Typeset by Ramesh Kumar Pitchai

Thank you

We rarely travel alone.

Many people have been involved with bringing this book into being; from people who were prepared to indulge me in endless conversations about the core ideas, to people like Diana Lodge, Rachel Nattrass and Angie Joint who had a much more hands on role in converting the ideas into a workable manuscript, and Jennifer Metcalfe who kept telling me I could get the project finished.

To one and all... a heartfelt thanks for helping me on my journey.

Paul

Contents

Foreword by Charles Jennings

High performance is all about performance and productivity. Effective learning is the way we deliver both.

However in our world where change is the norm it has become increasingly clear that most learning approaches are not working. The traditional understanding of what people need – usually expressed as 'knowledge' and 'skills' – and how they acquire it – usually in the form of structured courses and programmes – is failing to deliver the capability and performance needed.

We need new ways to approach both old and new problems. The old problem is that of ensuring our workforce delivers the value we need at the time we need it. The new problem is that of ensuring our workforce is both efficient and effective at learning, unlearning and re-learning in increasingly complex working environments at a speed faster than ever before.

In his '*Informal Learning at Work*' book, Paul Matthews wrote about the increasing importance of exploiting intangible assets in organisational success. As the workforce is the major intangible asset in any organisation it follows that agile and effective learning is a critical component in this process. Without agile and effective learning, and the ability to use the capabilities that develop from that learning, any workforce will not deliver optimum value.

In this new book Paul focuses on the performance puzzle. The answer to this puzzle, he argues, lies not so much in the process of learning (although how learning is achieved is critical) but in a laser-like focus on the outputs of learning – on effective capability and performance. It's what people can do and how well they can do it that counts. Whether they have passed tests to demonstrate levels of knowledge are merely secondary factors.

Moving from 'knowing' to 'doing is often a challenging task. In research for their ground-breaking book '*The Knowing-Doing Gap*', Stanford University academics Bob Sutton and Jeff Pfeffer found that most companies suffer from an inability to convert what they know into effective action. Even when organisations know what needs to be done they often experience an 'implementation shortfall'.

In this book Paul provides a detailed analysis of the knowing-doing challenge. He cites output from numerous studies and provides plenty of practical examples. Paul explains why traditional training has failed to build adequate capability and has subsequently failed to close the knowing-doing gap. He then discusses a series of approaches that can overcome the challenges and deliver capability at the 'speed of business'.

The solution Paul offers is not a simple one, but that's not surprising. The problem is large and complex, and simple solutions rarely emerge from such problems. However, the solution is a practical one. Paul draws on the excellent work of people such as Nigel Harrison, Geary Rummler and many others in providing this advice. It requires focus on new mindsets, new ways of approaching performance and productivity problems, new L&D roles and capabilities (particularly performance consulting capability), and new relationships between L&D and their stakeholders. Paul provides a roadmap to get there.

I found the insights in this book had me nodding my head in agreement on almost every page. The practical advice is clear and implementable, so long as the mindsets are primed. I am sure readers will want to keep it close at hand as they help their organisations meet the increasing demands for high performance from their workforces.

Charles Jennings
Winchester
August 2014

Chapter 1

Survive and thrive with capability

We are in the performance business, not the knowledge-gain business. The learning leaders who understand the difference are the ones who succeed.

Bob Mosher

This thought experiment reveals a lot: imagine for a moment that you're the chief executive of a new business, and you are offered a choice of two teams to work in your business.

Team one consists of people who are well-educated, have been on many training courses, and know a lot. They have degrees. They have certificates. They've attended all the best industry training courses. They are extremely knowledgeable in the areas in which the business will operate.

The second team is different. They aren't as well-educated but they all have a demonstrable track record in the industry. They are 100 per cent capable of doing the work that needs to be done in the new business.

Which team would you choose?

The knowledgeable team or the capable team?

It's a question that I've asked CEOs, company directors, and managers, as well as people in Learning and Development (L&D) and Human Resources (HR), in both the public and private sectors.

How did they answer?

Ninety-nine per cent picked Team Two, the capable team.

Why?

They all knew that in the moment when a job needs to be done, capability to do the job counts far more than the amount of training someone has done or even the amount of knowledge they possess. If you want your business to succeed, capability trumps knowledge.

At this point in the conversation, the L&D people often point out that all the knowledge of the people in Team One means they are, in effect, already capable. It is this blurring of the lines between knowledge and capability, or learning and capability, which leads to significant problems in the relationship between L&D and the people on the operational side of the organisation. More about this later.

Although this book is highly relevant to managers at any level in an organisation, I will assume the primary audience is people in L&D, HR, training functions, people development, or anybody in an organisation responsible for learning. Much of the book is about building an effective relationship between people in learning functions and people in operations, and so it is equally valuable to line managers when they need to interact with L&D.

In this book, you'll discover the importance of capability to organisational performance and why L&D and HR, and in fact every department, must make the capability of people and the capability of the organisation a priority if they want it (and their jobs) to survive in the current and future economy.

You'll see why focusing on performance and results rather than learning or training is key to business survival and why it's a mistake for L&D, HR and

Training to continue to focus only on their traditional core activities of creating content and delivering training.

You'll discover the key roles that L&D and HR should be playing in developing capability to improve individual and organisational performance, and the practical steps you can take within your organisation to start or enhance this process.

You'll learn the fundamentals of a systems view of organisational performance and the critical roles that HR and L&D have in organisational design and development.

You'll find out how you can move away from the passive and often ineffective role of training order-taker to become a major, and trusted, player in improving organisational performance.

You'll see why HR and L&D need to learn to speak and understand the language of business and put an end to the isolation professionals within such roles often experience.

You'll also find out the five critical components of capability and the important role each plays in any organisation's success.

Before we get into all of that, and given the title of this book, it's important to define what we mean by capability. My research and discussions with senior executives, business owners, managers and L&D and HR people has revealed that the concept of capability means different things to different people. That alone can cause major problems for any organisation.

For instance, many people tend to use the words 'competence' and 'capability' interchangeably, as if they are the same thing. They're not.

Capability versus competence

For the purposes of this book, competence is defined as the quality or state of being functionally adequate or having sufficient knowledge, strength and skill. Competence is another word for an individual's know-how or skill. A competent person has a demonstrable level of competence to perform a task, activity or function at a benchmark level.

When we ask whether someone has the right competencies, we're really asking, 'Do they know how?' and 'How well do they know?'

On the other hand, capability is the capacity of being able to perform actions.

The relevant questions for capability are not 'Do they know how?' but 'How can we get done what we need to get done?' and 'How easy is it to access, deploy or apply the competencies required for this task?'

The difference between capability and competence is significant.

There are many definitions of both capability and competence in literature and often they are somewhat self-serving, in the sense that they support the viewpoint or outcomes of the article or academic paper where they reside. They can also be somewhat complex, or offer a utopian view of what the words should mean in an ideal world.

I have a more simplistic approach in that I am concerned with how the words are used on a day-to-day basis. Here is a thought experiment to illustrate this:

Imagine for a moment that your car suddenly develops a strange noise under the bonnet. Strange noises in the engine can be very expensive to put right, so you know that you will have to take it to the garage as soon as possible to find out what is wrong.

At the time, like many parents, you are on a taxi journey taking your young son to football training, and he is very excited. It is the highlight of his day. Nevertheless, you detour to the garage after reassuring your son that you will still be able to get to football practice on time, and explain the problem to one of the mechanics who has serviced your car many times before.

As soon as he hears the noise he tells you he knows exactly what's wrong with your car, and that he can repair it. A small and inexpensive part has cracked and needs to be replaced. Better yet, he tells you it will only take ten minutes to do this, and he can do it straight away. Breathing a sigh of relief, you tell him to go ahead and repair the car and then you head off towards the waiting room with your son.

You've hardly had the chance to check your phone before he's back in front of you. 'That was quick,' you think before noticing the frown on his face. 'Something wrong?'

He looks apologetic. 'Well, I know I told you I can fix it but I've just checked and we don't have the spare part in stock right now, and according to the computer we can't source one locally. I can order it, but it'll take two days to come from the factory in Germany. I'm really sorry about that, we should have had the part in stock. I will come to your house and fit it for free as soon as it arrives. In the meantime I would not drive your car too far because that fault could get much worse and cost a lot more to put right. You should take your car straight home and leave it there until we can come and repair it.'

Maybe you take your car straight home, or perhaps you look for another garage where they may have the spare part in stock. Either way you are driving away from that garage with a car that is still broken and a son in the back seat who is very, very annoyed that he is going to miss football practice.

My question to you as you drive away is 'Was the mechanic capable of repairing your car? Yes or no?'

What is your answer?

I highly recommend that you try this thought experiment with your colleagues, your friends and anybody you can get to stand still long enough to listen. The responses you get are very enlightening because they vary depending on the viewpoint of the person you are speaking to.

Anybody with a business focus, such as an operational manager, business owner, managing director or entrepreneur, will say quickly and emphatically 'No! The mechanic was not capable of repairing the car.'

People in L&D and HR typically stop and think, and then say 'Yes, the mechanic was capable of repairing the car', or 'I don't have enough information to know if he was capable'. They often have difficulty in viewing the capability of the mechanic from the perspective of the business, or the customer. If I ask them to consider what answer the child in the back seat would give, they start to realise there are other ways to view the situation. What answer would the young football star give to the question about whether the mechanic was capable?

All the child knows is that he cannot go to football practice and, as far as he is concerned, the mechanic is responsible, because the mechanic was not capable of repairing the car when he was asked to.

Now, if you had asked the mechanic if he was competent at solving the type of problem your car has, he would have said 'Yes'. If you'd given him a test on repairing the fault on a car like yours, he'd probably have passed with flying colours. You know, too, that he was motivated to do the repair.

But from your viewpoint as a customer, all that matters is that he was not capable of repairing your car when you wanted it done. The fact that he was competent, motivated, engaged and had the required knowledge is immaterial, because he couldn't repair your car at the moment you wanted it repaired.

In other words, from your perspective as a customer, he was not capable.

There is a clear difference between how L&D and HR typically use the concept of the term capability compared with the other stakeholders in the business or the customer. In fact, they are actually answering a very different question, which is 'Could the mechanic repair the car?' This is much more about competence than capability – and the question does not include the context within which the task needs to be done. They rarely say 'That person may be competent but they are incapable of doing the job they need to do'.

I hope you can begin to see how this mismatch in the way different parts of the organisation use the concept of the term capability can lead to all sorts of problems. Critically, for our purposes, it causes some of the dissatisfaction that shows up when business managers are surveyed about the effectiveness of L&D functions.

This book is all about how to deal with the concept of capability, and how L&D people can alter their view of it so they can better align their activities with the business and get all the benefits which this brings to both L&D and the business.

Given that L&D is present to serve the business, and the business is present to serve the customer, it makes sense to define capability in this very simplistic way: if a worker can do the task at the point of work, they are capable. The task will get done and the desired results will be achieved for the customer, whether internal or external. If they cannot do the task at the point of work, for whatever reason, they are incapable.

Notice that my definition of capability only has meaning when it is coupled with the immediate work context; that is, it is only relevant at the point of work. The phrase '@ the point of work' was coined by Gary Wise[1] who is the Performance and Learning Solutions Strategist at Intellinex – a Xerox Company.

Given that any organisation has a purpose, and achieving that purpose is dependent on the people in the organisation being capable of doing all the tasks that need to be done at the point of work, capability is fundamental to success.

The capability agenda is far bigger than HR and L&D people think it is, and HR and L&D need to step up to this and think of capability in the way that the business does, and the way that customers do.

The components of capability

When you look at capability from the wider business perspective, you can start looking at it in terms of the components that are brought into play when an employee responds to a task in front of them.

For employees to be capable in the moment, at the point of work, the different components of capability must be at or over a threshold at which the employee can do a specific task at a specific time.

Those components consist of things that HR and L&D know well, such as knowledge, skills, mindset, attitude, motivation and engagement. But, as we can see from the example of the mechanic, capability at the point of work is also dependent on factors in the worker's environment, such as access to resources (the availability of spare parts, in the mechanic's case), access to the right tools, and access to just-in-time information. It is also dependent on the way they are managed, and the systems and processes that should deliver what the employee needs while they are doing the task.

Why is capability so important?

If we use our simple definition of capability, in order for anything to get done at all, the people being tasked to do it must be capable. They must be able to respond to the task in front of them adequately. This is at the heart of the performance agenda. If there is any kind of performance problem, or indeed any kind of issue at all within an organisation, you can trace it back to someone who was not capable of doing what they were asked to do. The root cause could, of course, be several steps removed from the apparent, and customer visible point of lack of capability. For example, the mechanic and his missing spare part may well be traceable back to a badly-programmed software system that was managing stock reordering levels, or poor management by the spares parts department manager.

Gloria Gery[2] in her book on performance support characterised the 'performance zone as the place where…

> "things come together… where people 'get it', where the right things happen, where the employee's response exactly matches the requirements of the situation… where employees put together all the individual [and collective] dance steps that they have mastered. The dance, the dancers, and the music are one."

Performance, and therefore capability have never been as critical as they are today, when many businesses and other organisations are struggling amid the global financial crisis to maintain performance and secure their economic future. Even government-funded public sector organisations have discovered that they are not immune to commercial realities. Throughout this book I will talk about the 'business', and by that I simply mean the operations part of an organisation – the part that is doing the work of serving customers, or patients, or constituents, or students, or anybody else who uses their products and services, whether paid for or not.

Clearly it is vital that everyone in the business has the capability to do the jobs in front of them at any given moment. Now set this requirement against the backdrop of the rate of change in today's world.

In today's business environment, change happens more frequently and faster than ever before. Peter Senge[3] described it this way in his book, *The Fifth Discipline…*

> "For the first time in history, humankind has the capacity to create far more information than anyone can absorb, to foster far greater interdependency

than anyone can manage, and to accelerate change far faster than anyone's ability to keep pace."

Detailed planning is difficult if not impossible. Today's business environment is Volatile, Uncertain, Complex and Ambiguous to borrow the term VUCA from the US military.

Companies, and their people, need the ability to respond, adapt and innovate even faster than the rate of change. They need to unlearn and relearn, and those that don't have that ability are destined to take a back seat or, worse, disappear completely from the marketplace. It is quite startling when you consider the list of large and seemingly stable organisations that have foundered or disappeared in the last couple of decades: Kodak, ICI, General Foods, AOL Time Warner, Wang, RCA, HMV, Jessops, Comet Group, Habitat, Borders, Nortel, Allied Carpets, Woolworths, Lehman Brothers, MG Rover, Arthur Andersen, Saab Cars, Daewoo and Barings Bank are a few examples. Not all of these collapses were simply the result of lack of innovation, but this was a major factor. It was the lack of ability to adapt to the VUCA world that allowed or led to other behaviours that brought the organisation to its knees.

The organisation was unable to perform well enough to survive. Ultimately, when you are talking about performance, you are talking about capability, and vice versa. Employees who are capable, according to our simple definition, deliver good performance, and performance is what the business is interested in. Indeed, performance is what is needed for the organisation to survive.

Globally, executives believe they need a 20 per cent improvement in their team's performance to meet their financial targets over the next 12 months, according to the Corporate Executive Board (CEB), a publicly-traded company that provides advisory services to businesses worldwide.

In an Executive Guidance report[4], the CEB said...

"Employee trends suggest employees are reaching a limit to their workload, but executives need a 20 per cent lift in workforce productivity.

"Many business leaders believe employees can be more productive. On average, executives think that only about 29 per cent of their employees are operating at peak productivity. Moreover, for every executive that believes his or her staff is fully productive, seven believe their staff could substantially improve."

Unfortunately, many employees are suffering from low engagement and stress – hardly the states to produce increases in productivity.

Only 13 per cent of employees worldwide are engaged at work, according to the State of the Global Workplace Study[5], Gallup's 142-country study. In other words, one in eight workers out of about 180 million employees in the countries studied are committed to their jobs and likely to make positive contributions to their organisations. It follows that about 63 per cent of the worldwide workforce are not engaged, meaning they lack motivation and are less likely to put effort into achieving their organisation's goals or outcomes. That leaves about 24 per cent of the worldwide workforce who are actively disengaged or unhappy and unproductive at work and liable to spread negativity to other employees. According to Gallup, this translates into 900 million full-time and part-time employees worldwide who are not engaged and 340 million who are actively disengaged. Little wonder then, that the global economy is struggling to recover from the economic downturn.

A 2011/2012 report from the UK's Health and Safety Executive (HSE) shows that work-related stress caused workers in Great Britain to lose 10.4 million working days in 2011-12. A widely reported estimate is that stress costs US businesses about $300 billion annually, due to absenteeism, lowered turnover, diminished productivity and medical, legal and insurance costs.

What all this research shows is that whatever measures have been taken in the past to boost performance on an individual and organisational level have not worked as they should – if indeed they ever did.

Writing in CEB's *Learning Quarterly magazine*[6], Thomas Handcock and Warren Howlett claim that unfortunately today's learning solutions won't deliver "more than a four per cent improvement in employee performance without some fundamental changes".

This is borne out by UK research that shows UK employees, managers and leaders lack the skills, knowledge and expertise necessary to do the jobs in front of them.

In 2012, for example, the UK's Department of Business, Innovation & Skills (BIS) and leading stakeholders, including the Chartered Institute of Personnel and Development (CIPD), produced a report[7] which found that the UK's competitiveness and performance were being held back by a lack of management and leadership skills.

In particular, the report noted that:

- Nearly three quarters of organisations in England reported a deficit of management and leadership skills in 2012, and that deficit is contributing to the UK's productivity gap with countries such as the US, Germany and Japan
- Incompetence or bad management of company directors causes 56 per cent of corporate failures
- Ineffective management is estimated to be costing UK businesses over £19 billion per year in lost working hours
- 43 per cent of UK managers rate their own line manager as ineffective – and only one in five is qualified.

The fortunes of an organisation can be transformed with skills such as people management, strategy and planning, budgeting and risk management, the report said, but added...

"Evidence shows that in general – both in the public and private sectors – the UK falls behind key competitor nations such as the US and Germany in terms of leadership and management capability. This is having a negative impact on the UK's competitiveness and performance.

"This is not a universal problem. The UK does develop some excellent managers and many organisations already benefit from successful approaches to building their management cadre, particularly multi-nationals and large corporates with significant HR functions.

"However, the evidence suggests that one of the fundamental problems holding back the growth of smaller and medium-sized organisations is a lack of leadership and management capability to drive performance and enable them to succeed."

According to another 2012 report[8], this time from the UK Commission for Employment and Skills, the UK's overall competitiveness is static, despite its "leading businesses being world class and the UK being a strong international economic force".

The World Economic Forum's Global Competitiveness Report ranks the UK economy as the tenth most competitive in the world, which remains lower than pre-recession rankings.

The UK's employment and productivity rates are "also not amongst the highest leading nations", the UK Commission for Employment and Skills pointed out.

Like the BIS report, it acknowledges that much progress has been made over the past decade in growing the skills of the workforce in the UK. It states...

> "Indeed, we have increased those with higher qualifications (at a degree level or above) by more than half, and reduced those with no qualifications by a third. We have also been moving to a more highly skilled economy..."

But progress obviously needs to be faster. According to the report...

> "Whilst our skill levels are increasing, they are not increasing fast enough relative to other leading nations around the world (we trail behind countries such as USA, Japan, Korea, Canada, Denmark, Norway, Finland, and the Czech and Slovak Republics) and at current rates we are set to fall further behind."

To be able to stay one step ahead of competitors and ensure their business survival, UK companies need to ensure they participate in an ongoing search for continuous improvement, operational excellence and high performance, the Commission says. It continues...

> "This places even more importance on the need for UK businesses to search for differentiation in products and services to meet changing consumer needs and to secure a continuing competitive edge."

Skills have a vital role to play to enhance business success, it says. The benefits associated with a higher skilled workforce include

- Improved productivity
- Better returns
- Increased employee satisfaction
- Lower rates of absence and staff turnover.

Employers with more highly skilled employees become more confident about their ability to adapt, which in turn encourages greater investment and innovation.

Persistent skills deficiencies, however, damage a firm's performance, the report notes, giving the example of manufacturing firms that were operating below full capacity and reporting skills gaps, and that were consequently only half as productive as other firms.

Higher productivity benefits the UK economy, the report said, explaining that a one percentage point rise in productivity or employment generates an additional £10 billion gross domestic product.

The BIS report emphasises the necessity for companies throughout the UK to improve leadership and management capability. It states...

"Quite simply, improving leadership and management capability is an issue that no organisation wishing to achieve long-term success can afford to ignore.

"There is no question that good leadership and management can have a truly significant impact on organisational performance, both in the immediate and longer term."

To illustrate the point, the report gives the following information:

- Best-practice management development can result in a 23 per cent increase in organisational performance
- Effective management can significantly improve levels of employee engagement
- A single point improvement in management practices (rated on a five-point scale) is associated with the same increase in output as a 25 per cent increase in the labour force or a 65 per cent increase in invested capital.

Commenting on the BIS report, the Chief Executive of the CIPD, Peter Cheese[9], said...

"There are eight million people in the UK workforce with direct management responsibility for one or more people. This army of people managers has a huge impact on this country's productivity and global competitiveness – not to mention on individual and social wellbeing and resilience.

"Leadership can no longer be about a few charismatic 'masters of the universe' at the top. There's a whole cadre of managers in the middle and on the front line who need to be equipped and inspired with the skills to lead and to win hearts and minds – from the very earliest stages of their careers.

"We can't as a nation afford to keep promoting people to management roles and assuming that these capabilities come naturally. We need a step change in the UK in how we develop and promote people management in every organisation, as this report so clearly highlights."

Although the reports quoted above are based on UK data, the conclusions drawn are not unique to the UK and are relevant to many other countries. No country or organisation can afford to be complacent about performance.

More often than not, organisations perceive good or strong performance as being evidence of a highly trained, knowledgeable and perhaps an engaged workforce, even though it may have had just as much or more to do with other factors, such as excellent goals, design and management of processes, systems or organisational structure.

Likewise, when performance and profits haven't met expectations, companies tend to identify a lack of training, knowledge and perhaps a lack of engagement as the reasons for the shortfall, when it could have been other factors, such as poor goals, design or management of processes, systems or organisational structure.

In many cases, organisations are trying to force performance improvements by investing in either learning or engagement initiatives, or both, when in reality those performance problems that are present are often a product of systemic failures. Learning and engagement programmes, therefore, are often the wrong tools to fix the apparent malaise.

Training: the knee-jerk reaction

When companies want to improve performance and results, often the knee-jerk reaction is to call for more training. The department responsible for training – whether it's called Learning and Development (L&D), Human

Resources (HR) or Training – is tasked to find an appropriate training programme to overcome the lack of performance, whether that's for employees, line managers or senior managers.

If that doesn't work, companies don't take a step back to determine the real reason for the performance shortfall. Instead, they are more likely to tell the HR or L&D departments to change the training programmes, find new training providers or to insource or outsource the training.

While all that is going on, there's a strong chance that the real reasons for the problem in performance will continue to damage the organisation's results.

In the Towards Maturity report *New Learning Agenda*[10], they state that...

> "...top learning companies are more driven by business priorities than others and involve business leaders directly with learning decisions rather than making them in isolation. Top learning companies are almost twice as likely to agree that:
>
> * they analysed the business problem before recommending a solution
> * they work with senior managers to identify specific business metrics to be improved
> * the business leaders recognised that learning is aligned with the overall business plan."

They go on to state...

> "Only 36% of organisations are working with business leaders to identify the business metrics that need to be improved through learning, with less than half of those businesses going back to review progress against the agreed metrics."

The failure of training programmes to improve performance will dent the confidence of the C-suite, managers and employees in the ability of HR, L&D or Training to contribute to the company's success, even if the cause of the problem had little to do with those departments.

To illustrate that point, let's go back to the mechanic from our thought experiment – the one who didn't have the spare part to do the job. Imagine that you aren't alone in your annoyance with the garage and, like other long-term customers, you are taking your business elsewhere. It's a fair bet that none of you really care about the reason for the mechanics' inability to do their jobs – you all just want the job done. If the mechanics can't sort out your problem, you will go elsewhere.

If the manager or owner behaves like the majority of managers and owners, he will see the resultant drop in revenue (from all the lost jobs), he will receive complaints from unhappy customers, and decide the problem lies with the mechanics.

'We're losing sales because the mechanics obviously don't know how to deal with customers. Right, let's get someone in to give them customer service training.'

The mechanics may or may not need customer service training. But a lack of customer service wasn't what was causing the drop in sales. If you recall, the mechanic in the story even offered to deliver the part and repair the car for free, acknowledging that the part should have been available. The real cause of the lack of capability, and therefore the performance problem, was that the garage's mechanics didn't have the resources they needed at the moment they needed them to carry out repairs.

So unless the root cause is addressed – in this case, a problem with spare parts inventory – the training the mechanics get in customer service will have almost no bearing on the results they achieve. Perhaps they will be able to communicate with customers in a way that fosters great relationships, but they still won't satisfy the customers' needs unless they have the spare parts they require to fix customers' cars.

Chartered business psychologist and performance consultant Nigel Harrison calls the rush to find quick fixes and instant solutions 'solutioneering'.

"Instant solutions are never successful on their own," says Harrison in his book, *Improving Employee Performance*[11]. He says, "The only way to guarantee success is to understand the causes of the real performance problems and implement integrated solutions."

Training does not breed good performance

The myth of training as the solution to poor performance has been reinforced by training departments over the years in support of their trade. They have 'sold' this idea to their senior teams for many years and it's a very seductive proposition which goes something like this:

Our workers (we will resist calling them human resource units) are not performing adequately, therefore there must be something wrong with them. They obviously don't know how to do their jobs, so we need to push knowledge and skills into them to remedy this deficiency. When they have this knowledge and these skills, they will perform better.

And by the way, if they don't perform better after attending training, it is again obvious that the training has not been comprehensive enough. They need longer training.

Perhaps we can even add in some special effects using accelerated learning techniques or days outdoors. If even that does not work, then sadly, we will need to consider hiring new workers who can be trained to do the job.

Many people in Training even believe it. But it is not true.

As an analogy, consider what a pharmaceutical company must provide by way of evidence before it can bring a new drug to market. Data need to be obtained from real patients that show beyond a reasonable doubt that the drug does, in fact, do what it claims to do. Given the number of variables present within patients undergoing a drug trial, getting hard data to prove drug efficacy is no simple thing. Nonetheless, the drug company has to design and execute an evaluation that unequivocally supports its claims, these difficulties notwithstanding. Before these regulations were in place, 'snake oil salesmen' were able to make any claim they wanted in order to sell quack remedies to the gullible.

The training delivered in so many organisations is never measured for its impact on downstream performance. What would be the result if purveyors of training had to execute an evaluation that unequivocally supported their claims?

A 2003 meta-analysis (an analysis of several studies of training practice) by Arthur, Bennett, Edens, and Bell[12], concluded that 78 per cent of all training is assessed for satisfaction. But their study also found that just 38 per cent of programs are evaluated for learning, nine per cent for transfer, and only seven per cent for the impact. Given such a low level of evaluation for the efficacy of the solution, would you buy the snake oil?

But often senior management asks for training as a knee-jerk response to performance issues, because they still believe in the myth. The 'jug and mug' approach (in which the teacher or trainer is regarded as the 'full jug' who can metaphorically pour their knowledge into the student or trainer, the 'empty mug') was sold to them right from when they started school at age five and experienced education. The schoolchild was told to sit still and be quiet in class and that, as a result, he would be successful.

Kandy Woodfield[13] on her blog put it like this...

> "All too often we ask people to join us in the classroom for a single one-off 'hit' of training, we take them from crawling to walking in one fell swoop and sometimes we don't even bother to ask if or why they want to learn to walk. For some people that's a bruising, scary experience and it's no wonder they fall over when they're back in their jobs, the learning experience is so ephemeral or awful that the skills, knowledge and behaviours mentioned are half-remembered but rarely acted upon. L&D needs to step up to its role in supporting holistic development rather than just providing training."

Managers have this idea that training is the answer, when in effect what they are trying to do is encourage people to change their behaviour through training. Behaviour change is certainly possible, but achieving this through training is extremely difficult. In the book *First Break All the Rules*[14], authors Marcus Buckingham and Curt Coffman detailed the results of two huge research studies undertaken by the Gallup organisation over a 25-year period. The studies involved over one million employees and 80,000 managers, and one of the findings was that "People don't change that much. Don't waste your time trying to put in what was left out. Try to draw out what was left in – that's hard enough!"

In her book *Turning Learning into Action*[15], Emma Weber says...

> "The only really effective way to change people is to encourage them and support them to want to make the change themselves. And yet a great deal of training is 'inflicted' on individuals who don't necessarily want to be in the training or don't understand why they are in the training. Making lasting change from that starting point is therefore extremely difficult. We cannot force someone to change, we cannot ask them to change and we cannot plead with them or cajole or punish them to change. We cannot

give them information and expect that they will automatically connect the dots and change work habits and processes that they have probably been using for years. And we certainly cannot remind people to change simply by bombarding the participant with an endless stream of content delivered in a variety of novel or innovative ways. Change is not the result of some magic bullet or fairy dust sprinkled over participants at the end of the course – it is a process, a measured and managed process. In fact the only similarity amongst the leading change methodologies is that everyone agrees that change is a process and that it occurs over a period of time. It is not an event. And self-change is infinitely more potent than administered change."

The importance of personal choice about change as opposed to enforcing change cannot be overemphasised. It is often said that people do not like change, but in reality what they don't like is change imposed upon them. People often create change in their own lives by moving jobs, buying a house, or having children.

In 1976, Ellen Langer and Judith Rodin conducted a famous study in a nursing home to assess the effects of enhanced personal responsibility and choice on a group of the nursing home residents. It was hypothesised that the debilitated condition of many of the aged residing in institutional settings is, at least in part, a result of living in a virtually decision-free environment and consequently is potentially reversible. Residents who were in the experimental group were given a communication emphasising their responsibility for themselves, whereas the communication given to a second group stressed the staff's responsibility for them. In addition, to bolster the communication, the former group was given the freedom to make choices and the responsibility of caring for a plant rather than having decisions made for them and the plant taken care of for them by the staff, as was the case for the latter group. Questionnaire ratings and behavioural measures showed a significant improvement in alertness, active participation, and a general sense of well-being for the experimental group over the comparison group.

A year and a half later the residents were retested and the first group was found to be more cheerful, active and alert. They were also healthier. Less than half as many residents from the first group died over the term of the experiment compared with the group who were not exerting any autonomy over their day-to-day lives.

Thankfully, many in L&D are now delivering interventions other than training that are required for performance, such as coaching, performance support and so on. The list grows ever larger as sections of the L&D community begin to question the traditional approach to training. Jenny Dearborn[16], Senior Vice President and Chief Learning Officer, SAP says...

> "Several recent studies have shown that our cognitive machinery is fundamentally incompatible with conventional, one-way schooling. The traditional one-to-many approach to teaching and learning isn't effective. The days when knowledge was considered a commodity to be delivered from teacher to student are over. Instead, knowledge emerges through curiosity-fueled exploration. Everyone must be a student and a teacher.

> "Corporate learning executives are bringing this approach to the workforce, shifting the focus from activity-based learning to experiential learning. By integrating interactions, mentoring, coaching, action-based learning, shadow assignments, and access to educational resources into the learning program, corporate learning can help employees feel empowered, invested, and engaged to the business."

One of the jobs facing forward-thinking L&D practitioners right now is to educate people at all levels in their organisations to dispel this pernicious myth of training as the magic bullet for performance problems. Unfortunately, many people in L&D see this as an activity that is a bit like a turkey voting for Christmas: a philosophy that challenges the need for training is seen by many as a threat to their own jobs.

L&D needs to face up to reality and realise that there are often restraining forces on performance that have a root cause which is neither lack of learning nor lack of engagement, although these factors are often present as well and get all the blame for the lack of performance.

Those factors, according to business improvement expert, Alan P Brache[17], could include...

- A weak strategy
- Poorly-designed business processes
- The misuse or non-use of technology

- Unclear or unwise policies
- Inadequate skills
- A dysfunctional culture
- An incentive system that rewards the wrong performance.

The interesting thing about this is that very often the workers themselves, when asked what frustrates them, already know what is slowing the system down and putting the brakes on performance.

And what is even more interesting is that very often removing these barriers to performance is a cheaper path to improving performance than trying to force through the barriers by applying learning and/or engagement programmes. Take the stones away from in front of the wheels and the cart will roll forward so much more easily.

When an organisation focuses on removing these restraining barriers and, in effect, enabling people to do their jobs more easily, higher levels of engagement will naturally follow. It is much easier to get enthused about a job when it is easy to do and you have all the tools with which to do it. And a natural progression from there is that people will actually seek to learn anything new that they need in order to continue working in this new and much more 'user friendly' environment.

I find it fascinating that organisations spend money, sometimes huge amounts of it, on leadership and engagement programmes because they feel these are the solution to dealing with their perceived performance issues. And yet alongside these leadership and engagement programmes there is little or no effort to better enable the workforce to do the tasks they are being asked to do. In my opinion organisations should start with enabling people; in effect, making them capable more often at the point of work. This in turn will have a more immediate and also lasting positive effect on engagement and productivity.

Good performance occurs when a number of things come together in the right order and at the right time, like the ingredients and the steps of a recipe.

Good performance happens when the performer is able to apply themselves to the task in front of them with the exact response required for the task, and within an environment that allows that response.

At the point of work the performer needs to be...

- Ready to do the task, while knowing they are ready and confident they have what it takes to succeed – readiness is as much about attitude as anything else, and that can indeed be a result of training, and also of practice or social learning from colleagues, or observation of experts.

- Knowledgeable – which can also be the result of training, although these days, with the rapid changes in knowledge, just-in-time support may often be a better option to introduce the knowledge ingredient.

  This is critical – an IDC global survey of information workers and IT professionals in the United States, UK, France, Germany, Australia and Japan, undertaken for Adobe[18], found that information workers waste a significant amount of time each week dealing with a variety of challenges related to working with documents. This wasted time costs organisations $19,732 (about £12,750) per information worker per year and amounts to a loss of 21.3 per cent in an organisation's total productivity. The report said that for an organisation with 1,000 people, addressing these time wasters would be tantamount to hiring 213 new employees.

- Skilled – which comes from repetitive practice of required behaviours, ideally in similar work contexts rather than role-plays in a training room

- Motivated – which comes from the engagement engendered by the leadership which surrounds them

- Networked – so that the performer can reach out to colleagues, the internet and other resources to ask questions and get answers

- Supported – so there is a sense of a safety net if things don't go as planned; in other words, there is risk management and contingency plans are in place

- Operating within a system that allows the performer to do what needs to be done. That is, systems, processes, inventory, resources and all the other 'hard' non-people components are also in place.

There is much more to performance than can be provided by training alone. Without the other ingredients that constitute capability at the point of work, your organisation and your people will simply never rise to the occasion.

The focus on training, learning and engagement are all red herrings, distracting not only L&D and HR, but often management, from what they should be focusing on.

A red herring (when used as an idiom) is a piece of information or suggestion introduced to draw attention away from the real facts of a situation. In reality, a red herring is a type of strong-smelling smoked fish that used to be drawn across the trail of a scent to mislead hunting dogs and put them off the scent. Don't get put off the scent. Focus on what is important: performance.

Fred Harburg wrote in the *Chief Learning Officer*[19] magazine...

> "Our customers have little interest in classes, learning management systems or blended learning. Their passion is for improved business performance, at the highest impact, with the lowest cost and in the least disruptive manner possible. If they could gain improvement through a special pill, magic potion or a silver bullet for a reasonable price, they would line up for it in droves. If you agree with this logic, then it follows that we are not in the business of providing classes, learning tools or even learning itself. We are in the business of facilitating improved business performance."

The business wants performance. Customers want performance. And actually, performance is what the workers want. It's my belief they would love to do a good job if only we would enable them to do so.

When I ask someone in L&D to reimagine their role so that their total focus is on ensuring capability at the point of work, their thinking changes. They start thinking in much more practical terms about how they can enable and help that worker do the job that is immediately in front of them. Some learning may be required, but often it will involve making other necessary changes to ensure capability at the point of work.

The same thing happens when I talk to HR people about moving their focus away from engagement and onto capability and thus performance.

There are many things that can be done to enable people without 'using' learning and engagement. Instead, give them the right tools, the right information, and processes that flow well. Put right the things that frustrate them. Take the brakes off what they are doing. Performance will improve.

I believe that when the brakes are taken off, and someone can do better, they will. They will also become more engaged and willing to learn, now they can see that better performance is possible. It wasn't them being stupid or not caring; it was the systems and processes and environment in which they were being asked to work that were preventing them from doing the good job they wanted to do.

Chapter 2

Changing your perspective

A man will be imprisoned in a room with a door that is unlocked and opens inwards as long as it does not occur to him to pull rather than push.

Ludwig Wittgenstein

Analysing a performance problem to determine the cause on any kind of scale – macro or micro – is not something the majority of HR and L&D professionals are usually asked or expected to do. Instead, they are usually told what the problem is and, more often than not, what the solution is – more training.

The solution is usually prescribed by the executive or manager who is responsible for the people who are not performing well. They rarely mention the gap in job performance or organisational results that have occurred because of the performance problem.

Instead, the conversation between executive/manager and the HR/L&D/ Training person usually goes something like this...

'It's Claire here... The Board believes the Finance team need leadership training. Can you take care of this? ... You can? Great! Can I leave it to you to put some recommendations on costings in a report so I can take it back to the Board next month? Thanks!'

Or this...

'Hi, it's Richard Dyer here. This is a message for Kate Hopkins. I've just came out of the divisional heads meeting and am about to go into another so I've only got a few minutes. We need some project management training because our teams are having a problem staying on budget. We need to start with the South-West and then roll it out to the EMEA teams. We've got preliminary approval. Can you give me a rough estimate for costs, timing and delivery? Okay, speak soon.'

People in HR and L&D are perceived as reactive and passive order-takers rather than proactive business partners.

These aren't conversations are they? They're instructions. We've met without you. We've decided what the problem is, and the solution. We're not sharing our thought processes on this with you. We're not even sharing the precise nature of the problem or what the impact of that problem is on the individuals involved or the company as a whole. What we want you to do is provide a training course on demand.

And yes, I know that this is not universal across all organisations. And yet it is depressingly common, even in organisations where the rhetoric is about business alignment and solving performance problems. In reality what is going on is still simple order taking for training/learning interventions.

In *How to be a True Business Partner by Performance Consulting*[20], Chartered Business Psychologist and Performance Consultant Nigel Harrison says...

"Depending on your perceived role (for example as 'Training Consultant', 'IT Consultant' or 'HR Consultant'), your client may expect you to be the person who will deliver their solution for them; and the first problem we often have to deal with is our client's expectation that we will merely take orders for their designed solutions.

"You can tell when a client perceives you as an 'order-taker' because they will give you very little time: for example 'I only have ten minutes, but

I just want you to...' (After all, if they only expect to pass on an order to you, it will not take very long!)."

The problem is that if you take the order and deliver the prescribed 'solution', there's a very strong chance it won't resolve the problem.

Harrison gives the example of an order-taker in action who is asked to organise a leadership course and readily agrees to do it. The only questions they ask are, 'How many people do you want to go on it?' and 'When do you want it done by?'

"Doesn't this business partner sound efficient? But the end result for the organisation is that 40 senior managers attend a 'leadership course' at a cost of £200k to the training budget, plus lost opportunity cost; and whilst the participants said they received value, there were no defined business benefits and no measurable value added to the organisation.

"In fact, the course distracted managers from their immediate business priorities. Later in the year, when the client has to call an emergency meeting to deal with business issues, the learning business partner [order-taker] is not invited because they are perceived only as 'the person who organises courses'."

In the early 2000s a British telecom provider found itself facing an image problem. Its aggressive sales tactics were winning huge volumes of business. Its lack of focus on customer care was aggravating a number of people who were beginning to become loud and vocal in the British press. The directors were advised by their marketing team that this had to be addressed.

The training and HR team were summoned and told to develop a customer care training course. They were told that the outcome had to be a positive one and that heads would roll if it was not. The training team duly got their heads down and developed an incredibly good customer care course. The program was rolled out across the organisation and was a resounding success in resolving the attitude towards customer care in the business.

It sounds like good news for this training team doesn't it? It wasn't. The average call time per operator contact increased dramatically. The company's profits were not made on a single sale, but rather on a volume bonus for selling a minimum number of connections a month. They actually took a small loss on each sale in order to remain highly competitive to attract the volumes of customers they needed. Their customers may have been happier, but there were fewer of them. The new approach slowed the sales people down to such an extent that the volume sales targets could not be met.

The program was scrapped. An embarrassed management team then had to encourage salespeople to forget the learning (always easier said than done) and focus back on high-speed turnover. The tiny vocal number of complainants in the media was offered the usual sweetener of a bottle of wine or a bunch of flowers and the PR crisis was averted.

Analysing the organisational system to determine the cause of a performance problem is critical and it's a skill that HR and L&D need to develop. It is not sufficient to only consider performance from the point of view of a person, a single team, a department, or a division.

Not doing so is the biggest mistake many organisations make where performance is concerned. People within teams, departments and divisions can become so blinkered about their area or function, they stop thinking of or seeing it as part of an organisation.

Instead, each team, department or division operates as a single entity rather than part of a whole organism. This micro-viewpoint, in which departments or divisions are perceived as separate entities, can result in a dysfunctional organisation.

Our telecoms provider didn't need a customer care course – it needed a solution to the PR issue. That was something that might have been spotted if the HR and L&D teams hadn't been reacting to fulfilling an order.

Here is another story which I have heard. I have no idea if it is true, but nonetheless it illustrates an interesting point. The scene was a packaging line in a factory that made toothpaste. Each tube of toothpaste was packaged in a small cardboard box before in turn being packaged up in boxes of 50 units. They received regular complaints from customers that some of the small cardboard boxes were empty. The complaints filtered back to the supervisor of that particular production line, but despite his best efforts to train and re-educate the people who operated the packing machine that inserted the tubes into the small boxes, the problem continued. Empty boxes still got onto the conveyor that headed off to the final packing area. The supplier of the packing machine insisted that it was working properly.

The engineers were called in, and they devised and built a special weighing point in the conveyor so that the occasional empty box could be identified and pushed off the conveyor with a little pneumatic arm. Each time this happened, a short alarm would sound. This expensive system worked perfectly, the empty boxes were discovered and discarded, and the alarm would go off about once an hour. One empty box an hour was considered acceptable.

Suddenly, after a week, the alarm stopped sounding. They checked to see if the fancy weighing machine was still working. It was. There were no empty boxes getting through to the last packing area. It was only then that they found a large fan which was propped up on a pallet facing the conveyor belt a few metres upstream of the weighing machine. A long-serving employee who kept that area tidy and swept the floor had become tired of the constant alarm sound. His solution was the fan which blew the empty boxes off the conveyor belt before they were discovered by that noisy weighing machine.

In their groundbreaking book, Improving Performance: *How to Manage the White Space on the Organization Chart*[21], Geary A. Rummler and Alan P. Brache say that optimal performance in one department or function can result in a fall in the overall organisation's performance. They say...

> "As each function strives to meet its goals, it optimises (gets better and better at 'making its numbers'). However, this functional optimisation often contributes to the sub-optimisation of the organisation as a whole."

For example, a marketing and sales department might reach its goal of selling thousands of units per quarter, but if the organisation's manufacturing and distribution departments aren't operating effectively, so that they can't make sufficient products, customers won't get the units they've ordered. That in turn could affect the company's cash flow and perhaps profits.

So although the sales department might reach its goal, it wouldn't improve the company's performance. It could even damage the organisation's reputation since customers would have to wait longer than they expected to receive the goods they'd ordered.

This focus on parts of an organisation is a problem of perception and it's one that can affect everyone, from the CEO to the workers at the front desk or on the production line. Many business managers and employees have a flawed perception of how their organisations actually work. They don't, for instance, have a detailed understanding of how their business develops or creates products or services, or how those products or services are sold and then distributed or delivered.

Typically, people within the business refer to the organisational chart as being representative of the way the company operates. While organisational charts are useful for defining the individuals and departments that make up the organisation, they don't show the interdependent nature of the organisation's components or how the work actually gets done.

For that you need to view the organisation as a system. A system is an entity that maintains its existence and functions as a whole through the interaction of its parts. Systems thinking looks at the whole, and the parts, and the connections between the parts, studying the whole in order to understand the parts. A collection of parts that do not connect is not a system. It is a heap.

When you look at the patterns that connect the parts rather than simply the parts themselves, a remarkable fact emerges. Systems made from very different parts having completely different functions follow the same general rules of organisation. Their behaviour as a system depends on how the parts are connected, rather than what the parts are. This means that you can make predictions about the behaviour of the system and the parts without knowing about the parts in detail.

Given the hugely complex systems surrounding us, an understanding of the general rules of organisation of those systems is clearly useful. There are many books on systems thinking, and most of those have a very strong academic flavour. One book that makes the subject rather more accessible is *The Art of Systems Thinking: Essential Skills for Creativity and Problem Solving,* by Joseph O'Connor and Ian McDermott.[22]

Looking at the system

According to systems theory, all organisations are systems and all systems are part of even larger systems.

A system is defined in two ways.

1. Externally, it is defined by its purpose – that is, every system plays a part in the higher level system in which it exists.
   If your organisation manufactures car parts, for example, it is a system which has a role to provide car parts to the next higher level system, car manufacturers. Those car manufacturers have roles to play in the next higher level system, the motor vehicle market. The motor vehicle market has roles to play in the higher level systems of transportation and the national economy and so on.

2. Internally it is defined by its subsystems and internal functions – each system is made up of components and subsystems that interrelate and contribute to the overall purpose of the parent system.
   With an organisation that manufactures car parts, for example, its components might consist of engineering, production, marketing, finance, sales, and human resources.
   All those components and subsystems should support the system's purpose of providing car parts to the higher system, the car manufacturers. If a subsystem can fit the needs of the larger system, it will survive. If it doesn't meet the needs of that larger system, it will wither and die.

So when considering performance issues, it's quite possible that it will be important to understand how your organisational system relates to the larger system in which it exists and operates. That larger system includes factors and forces that may include competitors, customers, suppliers, technological advances, consumer rights, social forces, local and national governments, government regulations, international governments and regulations, the national economy and the international economy, and environmental concerns.

It's also important to understand how your organisation's internal systems add to or detract from that larger relationship.

One way to understand systems theory is to think of the systems that operate within your body. As you read these words, your autonomic nervous system (one of the subsystems in your body) is regulating your body's involuntary actions, such as your heartbeat and digestion.

Your autonomic nervous system is part of a bigger system – the nervous system – which acts as your body's control system and sends, receives and processes the nerve impulses throughout your body. These nerve impulses tell your muscles and organs what to do and how to respond to the environment.

Your nervous system consists of the central nervous system, the peripheral nervous system, and the aforementioned autonomic nervous system.

The nervous system is one of a number of subsystems in your body, which operate independently and together.

Other subsystems include the circulatory system, the digestive system, the endocrine system, the immune system, the lymphatic system, the muscular system, the reproductive system, the skeletal system, the urinary system and the respiratory system.[23]

As with other systems, when one part of the human body is altered or changed, the entire system is impacted. When one part is replaced, the reverberations are experienced throughout the system and its functions will be affected, even if the new part is 'better' or 'healthier' than the old replaced part.[24]

Doctors study the systems running in the human body in such detail that they know how they interact with each other. They know which factors govern good health, and the impact of a failure of any of those factors, and also what needs to be done to correct the failure and return the patient to good health.

In his book, *Serious Performance Consulting*,[25] Geary Rummler says...

> "The physician also knows that symptoms in one area may result from problems in another: this understanding requires them to take a systems view of the problem.

> "Even though patients come in different sizes and colours, physicians know that inside, they all have the same parts, located in basically the same physical area, and that they are supposed to perform the same function within the system. The same is true with a business."

Like a physician, a performance consultant must understand the anatomy of the system he or she is examining – in this case, a business – and how the systems within it interact as well as the factors that govern good 'health' (strong performance and results). Only then can the performance consultant determine the real cause of any problem.

As different as businesses may appear in size or product/service, inside they all have a common anatomy.

According to Rummler...

> "In the eyes of a serious performance consultant, every performance issue – individual, job or process – must always be seen in the overarching organisational context: the anatomy of performance."

He says the anatomy of performance, boils down to the following two points...

1. An organisation is a complex system of individuals, jobs, processes, functions and management.
2. Organisational performance or results are a function of how well these interdependent components are aligned and working toward clearly specified results.

Unfortunately, too few managers have a deep enough understanding of their organisation's complex anatomy.

Rummler and Brache[26] say when they ask managers to describe their department, division or organisation, they are usually given a description that fits in with what managers have seen on an organisational chart – in other words, a description of the organisation's functions at each vertical level. They say...

> "The danger lies in the fact that when managers see their organisations vertically and functionally, they tend to manage them vertically and functionally. More often than not, a manager of several units manages those units on a one-to-one basis."

When that happens, goals are established for each function independently, and meetings between functions are limited to activity reports. Managers further down the line then tend to see other departments or divisions as separate rather than partners.

You get a situation where departments or divisions operate as if they exist in silos. Those silos prevent interdepartmental issues being resolved by peers at low and middle levels, say Rummler and Brache. Instead issues are escalated to the managers at the top of each silo for resolution at that level. Once the issues are resolved, they are communicated down to the level within the silo at which the work will get done.

Managers at the top levels of each silo are forced to resolve low-level issues, which in turn takes them away from higher priority concerns with competitors or customers, and overall strategy. The people who could be resolving those low level issues learn to take less and less responsibility for results.

Sometimes, cross-functional issues aren't even addressed but instead fall into the white spaces on the organisational chart. The issue does not have an 'owner' and so rumbles on never being addressed or resolved.

Taking a systems view of the organisation

Contrasting with the functional silo view of an organisation (which doesn't include the company's customers, its products or services, or the work flow that produces and delivers the products or services) is the systems view of the organisation, which includes how everything in the business' internal and external ecosystem (including customers, products and services, reward systems, technology, organisation structure and so on) are connected.

A systems view of an organisation shows you how work gets done through processes that cross functional boundaries and the internal customer-supplier relationships through which products or services are produced, as well as the flow of demand and supply.

"In our experience," say Rummler and Brache, "the systems view of an organisation is the starting point – the foundation – for designing and managing organisations that respond effectively to the new reality of cutthroat competition and changing customer expectations."

What's more, the greatest opportunities for performance improvement can often be found in the places where tasks or jobs are passed from one department to another. Those might include, for example, the transfer of client billing information from the sales department to the finance department or the passing of new product or service ideas from the marketing department to the research and development department.

Organisational and individual performance improvements happen only when there's a clear understanding of the connections in the organisation's internal and external systems.

Rummler and Brache recommend examining three levels of performance – the organisational level, the process level and the job/performer level.

1. Organisational performance is the performance desired by the business. Factors that affect performance at this level include strategies, organisational goals and measures, and the organisation's structure and deployment of resources.

2. Process performance is the performance required of all processes in order to achieve the organisation-level performance.
It is concerned with the organisation's cross-functional processes (production, order fulfilment, product development, complaint-handling,billing, planning, hiring, sales, distribution and so on). These processes should meet the needs of customers and stakeholders and must work effectively and efficiently. The goals and measures for all processes must be driven by the requirements of customers and the organisation.

3. Job performance is the performance required of all jobs in order to achieve the process-level performance.
It is concerned with how the work is performed and managed by individuals within the organisation. Factors that affect performance at this level include hiring, promotion, job responsibilities and standards, feedback, rewards, training and so on.

Ideally, the performance goals, structures and management actions at all three levels – organisational performance, process performance and job performance – are aligned.

How well the organisation performs (how well it meets the needs and wants of its customers) is the result of goals, structures and management actions at all three levels of performance, say Rummler and Brache.

1. Goals

   All three levels of performance need specific standards that reflect customers' expectations for product and service quality, quantity, timeliness, and cost.

2. Design

   All three levels of performance need structures that include the necessary components, configured in a way that enables the goals to be efficiently met.

3. Management

   All three levels of performance need management practices that ensure the goals are current and are being achieved.

It is important that all three levels are evaluated, since a change in one level will affect the performance of the other levels. Any performance improvement that doesn't include all three levels will likely result in piecemeal improvements at best.

How to improve performance

Managers at any level can use the nine variables (Organisation Goals, Organisation Design, Organisation Management, Process Goals, Process Design, Process Management, Job Goals, Job Design, and Job Management) as improvement levers, according to Rummler and Brache.

Whenever a performance improvement lever is pulled, it must always be remembered that it is part of a system. The three levels of performance are interdependent. That means, for example, that an attempt to introduce an organisational goal will fail if that goal is not supported by processes and human performance systems. Equally, a job can't be defined by someone who doesn't understand the needs of the business process that the job exists to support.

From this, it's clear that before performance at any of the three levels can be managed, the expectations for that performance need to be established and communicated.

It's also crucial that the purpose of the business is clearly defined and communicated throughout the organisation.

If the business is not clearly defined, it is almost impossible to design and manage not only the organisation level of performance, but also the structure and management practices at the process and job performer levels.

Without a clearly defined strategy, it is also very difficult to be certain that resources are being effectively allocated, that key business processes are being managed effectively, or that the correct job performance is being recognised and rewarded.

To define the business's strategy, executives and senior managers need to be clear on the following:

- What products or services the organisation offers
- What customers and markets it serves
- What competitive advantages it has over its competitors
- What its product and market priorities are
- That the systems and structures it has will produce the products and services it offers to its customers and markets at competitive advantages.

Once a business strategy is decided, it needs to be communicated throughout the organisation. Alongside this, an infrastructure needs to be established that supports the strategy implementation at all three levels: organisation, process and job/performer. Then it is about execution of the strategy, monitoring of results, and the inevitable iterative process of strategy and tactical activity improvement.

In an ideal world, executives and managers will take the time to ensure that the business purpose and strategy are clearly defined, that the system works effectively, and that all three levels of performance are working as they should.

Now, that might or might not be happening in your organisation, but it's important to find out if your organisation has clearly defined goals and strategy for each of the three levels of performance.

Hundreds of studies conducted in numerous countries and contexts have consistently demonstrated that setting specific, challenging goals can power-fully drive behaviour and boost performance.

However, be careful. In their paper; 'Goals Gone Wild: The Systematic Side Effects of Over-Prescribing Goal Setting' [27], Lisa Ordóñez et al caution against the indiscriminate use of goal setting without considering the larger system in which goals are used. They say...

"Rather than dispensing goal setting as a benign, over-the-counter treatment for motivation, managers and scholars need to conceptualize goal setting as a prescription-strength medication that requires careful dosing, consideration of harmful side effects, and close supervision."

They also offer a ten-point checklist for organisational goal setting to ensure that goals are supporting organisational objectives correctly. The checklist starts with a warning notice which says...

"Goals may cause systematic problems in organisations due to narrowed focus, unethical behaviour, increased risk taking, decreased cooperation, and decreased intrinsic motivation. Use care when applying goals in your organisation.

1. Are the goals too specific?
   Narrow goals can blind people to important aspects of a problem. Be sure that goals are comprehensive and include all of the critical components for firm success (e.g., quantity and quality).

2. Are the goals too challenging?
   What will happen if goals are not met? How will individual employees and outcomes be evaluated? Will failure harm motivation and self-efficacy? Provide skills and training to enable employees to reach goals. Avoid harsh punishment for failure to reach a goal.

3. Who sets the goals?
   People will become more committed to goals they help to set. At the same time, people may be tempted to set easy to reach goals.

4. Is the time horizon appropriate?
   Be sure that short-term efforts to reach a goal do not harm investment in long-term outcomes. For example, consider eliminating quarterly reports as Coca Cola did.

5. How might goals influence risk taking?
   Be sure to articulate acceptable levels of risk.

6. How might goals motivate unethical behaviour?
    Goals narrow focus, such that employees may be less likely to recognize ethical issues. Goals also induce employees to rationalize their unethical behaviour and can corrupt organizational cultures. Multiple safeguards may be necessary to ensure ethical behaviour while attaining goals (e.g., leaders as exemplars of ethical behaviour, making the costs of cheating far greater than the benefit, strong oversight).

7. Can goals be idiosyncratically tailored for individual abilities and circumstances while preserving fairness?
    Strive to set goals that use common standards and account for individual variation.

8. How will goals influence organizational culture?
    If cooperation is essential, consider setting team-based rather than individual goals.

9. Are individuals intrinsically motivated?
    Assess intrinsic motivation and recognize that goals can curtail intrinsic motivation.

10. Consider the ultimate goals of the organization and what type of goal (performance or learning) is most appropriate?
    In complex, changing environments learning goals may be more effective."

Goals are key to driving organisational performance. However, poor goal design is as likely to result in destructive performance as it is to achieve the results demanded by the external systems of clients and stakeholders.

The structures that need to be in place to enable the achievement of goals is the realm of organisational design. An organisation is made up of subsystems and they must be designed to work together in order to achieve the objectives laid down by the external systems. Many of the challenges faced by organisational designers relate to the interface between different business silos, and the information exchange across those interfaces.

In organisations where managers barely communicate with their peers in other sub-systems; it is highly unlikely that workers are reaching out across the divide. A leadership structure which pays lip service to cooperation, but demonstrates competition, will not engender a systems approach throughout the organisation.

Carol Rozwell[28] of the Gartner group says...

"There is much evidence to suggest that the same techniques used to train animals, either pets or performers, are just as effective with children, spouses and employees. What's the trick? Positively reinforce the behaviours you want to see continue. The corollary is also true: you need to model the behaviour you want others to exhibit.

"I raise this issue because in so many of my recent conversations with clients about the adoption of social software and collaboration tools, a huge disconnect emerges. Managers and team leaders say they want employees to 'play nice together' but then they actively discourage collaboration through actions, directives and metrics."

I suspect that we have all seen this kind of behaviour in the workplace. There is a disconnect between the stated goals of a business and the way in which the leadership approaches those goals. Capability within the workplace relies on management behaving consistently with the system's requirements as much as it relies on the worker behaving consistently. Congruence is important. 'Do what I say, not as I do' is a poor message to send a child; it is a much poorer message to send out to adult employees.

Although it's beyond the scope of this book to cover organisational design, I do recommend that you talk to the people in your organisation who are responsible for it. To read about how HR can lead an organisation design project, I recommend Naomi Stanford's book, *Organization Design: The Collaborative Approach* (Elsevier, Butterworth-Heinemann, 2005), which is aimed at HR professionals.

Chapter 3

The new role for L&D

We're moving to a world that focuses on performance and experience. There is a productivity and performance focus, rather than just a learning focus.

Charles Jennings

Given what you have read in the first two chapters, what part do you think L&D (or HR or Training) can play in creating an organisation that focuses on performance?

The first step is to ensure that YOU are focusing on performance, rather than learning or training, as your ultimate endgame. When you focus on performance, and the gap between current performance and desired performance, you are inevitably dealing with capability of both the organisation and the individual. A focus on performance means a focus on capability as we have defined it in this book: can the performer do the task in front of them at the point of work?

It is easy to say 'focus on performance (or capability)' but I have found that most people in L&D find it actually quite difficult to do in practice. They have become so focused on learning as their primary outcome that many conversations with the business stakeholders about subsequent performance are cursory, or are simply used as a way to help them design the content of their training course, and the course learning outcomes. As a result of this discussion, they claim the training course is 'aligned' with the business.

I say to people that L&D is changing, and needs to change, and they all nod their heads and says yes, but when I look at what they're actually doing, it is clear that they are not taking that realisation to heart. They are not really modifying what they are doing sufficiently quickly to keep up with what's going on around them.

Clark Quinn somewhat provocatively starts Chapter 1 of his book *Revolutionize Learning & Development: Performance And Innovation Strategy For The Information Age*[29] with the following...

> "Let me be blunt: the current state of the learning & development (L&D) industry is failing. Badly. Overall, L&D is only doing a fraction of what it could and should be doing, and the part that is doing, it is doing poorly. The L&D industry has, by and large, been in denial and a willing participant in complacency. As a consequence, L&D is on a steady path to extinction. The perception of L&D's value to the organisation is largely one of irrelevance."

He goes on to say...

> "Yet the potential is there, particularly in this emerging age of change, for L&D to be perhaps the most essential component of a business. This mismatch between potential and current statuses is, quite simply, disheartening."

The core of the problem is that most L&D people are still content to define objectives 'at the end of this programme', when in fact it is not sufficient that people attend a training programme to acquire knowledge and skill. What ultimately matters is that these individuals apply the skills on the job so that their performance improves and the business consequently benefits. High quality learning and training do not necessarily translate into business results. In other words, the finishing line for learning is not at the end of the programme, but much later, on the job, after learning transfer.

An effective programme will have objectives defined in terms of on-the-job behaviours and business results; less effective programmes merely define what will be learned or covered on the course. So break free of your focus on learning outcomes. Within an organisation, learning is essential only to the degree that it contributes more to performance than other allocations of scarce resources.

It is only when you work with others in your organisation to analyse the real causes of a performance problem, either current or anticipated, that you will be seen by the business as adding significant value. One operations director I spoke to said in frustration that the L&D people in his organisation are off in 'learning la-la land', and did not understand his real needs in meeting his key performance indicators. The L&D people saw everything as a learning problem, and the operations director saw everything as a performance problem.

He was unusual in that he recognised that learning was not necessarily the solution to his performance problems, and was thus frustrated when this was the only solution on offer from a blinkered L&D department. Unlike him, the vast majority of managers still automatically assume that if there is a performance problem, people need training and thus they do not ask for more than just training from their L&D people. This is one reason that many people in L&D are complacent. They are delivering the learning/training that is asked for and thus assume it is sufficient and that they are satisfactorily fulfilling their role.

They couldn't be more wrong. Just because your customers are only asking for learning/training does not mean that is all they really need from you. Henry Ford once said that if he asked his customers what they wanted, they would have said 'A faster horse'. He gave them the motorcar. Apple developed a tablet computer that people did not ask for, and now many people feel that their iPad is indispensable. You can incrementally improve what you provide your customers by asking them what they want. If you want to dramatically improve the way you serve your customers, you must look beyond what they are asking for and understand their world and what they need.

So what is it that managers in the business need from you that they don't know enough in order to ask for it? Remember that their overriding need is for performance, and meeting their key performance indicators. How can you help them, your customers, with performance?

When you are facilitating conversations on performance, you are acting as a performance consultant. This is a new and often unfamiliar role to people in L&D who have traditionally focused on training or learning. It can also be uncomfortable because of the way that people will react to L&D behaving differently. Nonetheless, despite the unfamiliarity and discomfort, in my opinion, becoming a performance consultant is the only way to keep L&D relevant to the business.

So how do you become a performance consultant?

You stop being an order-taker. You stop automatically accepting requests or demands for training. You encourage executives and managers to recognise that a performance problem won't necessarily be solved by a training intervention, which can really only deliver skills or knowledge (and history shows that many training courses that are delivered do not even do this at all well).

Doing things so differently might be an uncomfortable thought – after all, delivering training is what you and your department do, isn't it?

If training is the only thing your department delivers, I would guess that your department is undervalued and overlooked by the rest of the business, because training cannot solve many of the problems that companies have. It can't fix problems that are caused by a faulty business process, an ill-conceived goal and a myriad of other causes that have a negative impact on performance.

When you offer training as the panacea for all performance-related problems, you set yourself and your department up for failure. The more you do this, the less likely you are to have your opinions sought out by the C-suite. The more likely it is that you and your department will continue to be undervalued and overlooked.

If you are happy with this state of affairs and the future it offers you, then you might as well put this book down and continue as you are. If you want to start shifting your role towards that of performance consultant, then here is how you can do it.

The first step is to get your L&D and HR colleagues on-board with your new remit: performance consultancy.

The next time you or your colleagues receive a request for training, you need to query whether training is the answer to whatever the problem may be.

Let's say, for example, that you get a call or an email from the Sales and Marketing Director. She wants a leadership training programme. As usual, the conversation goes something like this...

'It's Sally here. My team needs a leadership training programme. Do you or your team have any space in the calendar in the next four weeks?'

Previously, your automatic response might have been something like this: 'I'm sure we do. Let me have a look...' This is, after all, a perfect order-taker response. Someone else identified the problem and chose the solution: training. All you had to do was accept the order and ask for the specifics.

As a performance consultant, however, you'll do things differently. This means that when the Sales and Marketing Director calls you and asks for a leadership training programme, your immediate response will no longer be, 'Of course. When would you like it?'

Instead, you'll quiz her to determine how she believes that training will affect the behaviours of employees in ways that will improve the performance of her sales team and the performance of the business.

"When responding to a request for training, the HRD professional must realise that the requester probably has not conducted a thorough analysis and most likely does not know the limitations of training as a performance improvement intervention," say Rummler and Brache[30]. "All he or she knows is that there is a feeling of pain."

The primary objective has to be to understand the performance context of the request. Only then can anybody determine whether training is needed and, if so, the specific objectives that the training should meet.

You need to determine what behavioural changes are needed and you do that by carrying out a needs analysis. Notice that this is a Needs Analysis. It is NOT a Training Needs Analysis (TNA) which presupposes that what is needed is training. If you still use the term TNA, then ban it from your vocabulary.

So your questions should be along these lines:

- Why do you think your team (or whoever is line for training) needs training?
- What behaviours do your team need to demonstrate?
- What is the problem?
- What is causing the problem? How do you know?
- Who is involved?
- What is happening now?
- What do you want to happen instead?
- What is the cost of the performance gap?
- What are the potential solutions to this problem?

There is much more detail on how to go about this needs analysis or performance consultancy process later in this book.

According to Tom Bird and Jeremy Cassell in their book *Business Training*[31], which is part of the Financial Times Guides series, "If you are going to undertake an effective needs analysis, you need to challenge, to look deeper into a presenting issue to ensure that what you deliver will make a difference in the work environment."

They say that if you do not conduct an effective needs analysis, you risk...

- Focusing only on the 'ability' component of an issue and not on what is needed to implement change
- Ignoring the real reasons for the issue, therefore only being able to come up with a partial solution
- Rushing to 'solution' rather than considering the real performance issues
- Assuming that your clients are 'performance experts'
- Not being seen as a 'performance expert' yourself
- Being seen as having tactical rather than strategic value to the business
- Operating in isolation from other departments
- Being considered as a 'quick fix'
- Being criticised for being palliative – relieving without curing
- Being seen as out of touch and therefore being side-lined from the business

- Being blamed when training is seen to be not working
- Being considered a cost centre rather than a profit centre
- Being unable to justify how you add value to the business
- Not being taken seriously
- Being the subject of budget cuts
- Not making a positive difference to the business.

Bird and Cassell go on to say that you should be questioning your view of your role within the business, and they offer some useful questions to ask yourself:

- Are you a training professional or a performance expert?
- Are you focused on training or on results?
- Are you a business support department or a function that is central to business results?
- Are you prepared to challenge to get to the root cause or do you simply respond reactively to a perceived need?
- Do you seek to question or simply gain agreement?
- Do you simply teach skills and impart knowledge or do you influence people to apply them in the workplace?
- Do you work in isolation or holistically?

In time, once you have established in the minds of executives and managers that you are no longer an 'order taker' and you are focused on performance, you and your department can be more proactive and initiate performance discussions with other departments.

Using the language of business, not L&D or HR

As a result of this change in perspective, you'll almost certainly begin to change your language. That's crucial, because talking the 'language of business' is a vital part of overcoming, not only the perception that anyone involved in L&D is an order-taker, or off in 'learning la-la land', but also the miscommunications that are so much a current part of the relationships between L&D and the C-suite.

Have you ever phoned an off-shore call centre and been frustrated to find that, while the person on the other end of the phone appears to speak English, you do not make sense to them and they do not make sense to you? If so, you're not alone. And if you are like most people, your immediate thought is 'I am the customer, it is their job to understand me, not my job to understand them.'

When you are in L&D, the operations part of your organisation is your customer. They have every right as a customer to expect you to communicate with them in a way that makes sense to them.

So often when learning professionals attempt to engage with the business, the language they speak is not understood by the stakeholders in other functions of the organisation. In turn, learning professionals struggle to understand the language used by other stakeholders. This is a recipe for failure for both 'sides'.

Instead L&D needs to communicate effectively in the language of the stakeholder, whether that involves speaking to them, writing proposals, giving presentations or delivering reports.

L&D professionals need the skills to present information in such a way that all the relevant stakeholders can buy in to the ideas and delegate the authority required to put them into action.

Rita Smith[32], Vice President of enterprise learning at Ingersoll-Rand says...

> "We're here for only one reason: to help drive business outcomes. We need to understand the business strategy, key strategic drivers, external threats, and financial metrics. We literally need to be bilingual, speaking the languages of both learning and business."

Here is a simple exercise for you to do. Get together with your L&D colleagues and write a list of words and phrases that you use regularly, and which could be misconstrued or used with a different meaning, or subtlety of meaning, by other parts of the business. Then do the same thing with people elsewhere in your business. Ask their help to go through any internal business cases or proposals you have prepared, and point out to you words or phrases that are seen by them as L&D jargon. Then ask the help of someone completely outside your business to look at the same documents.

You will be very surprised at the size of the list of jargon words and phrases. Words you think are obvious and in common usage are seen as jargon by others when you use them. Now go through that list and find out what word or phrase would be used by an operations manager to mean the same thing, if indeed they even have an equivalent concept for it. Remember that some words have a lot of semantic baggage attached to them, so even differences in nuance of meaning are important.

You should also do this exercise in reverse, and go through business plans or proposals put together by people in operations. Look for words that to you seem like business jargon. Make sure you understand their meaning as they are used generally in business, especially if they have a unique meaning in your own business. Many organisations develop a lexicon of acronyms, words and phrases that have special meaning within that organisation. This lexicon of jargon was not planned, but it has arisen as people sought ways to make communication within the organisation succinct and unambiguous. By all means use the internal jargon of the business, but be very certain that you know what it means to your audience. A large organisation can have localised jargon.

The business areas where L&D people are often lacking in understanding are those relating to the organisation's mid-term and long-term strategy, and those relating to finance. If these areas seem a bit irrelevant to you, think again. It is vitally important that you are able to converse about strategy and finance with the people to whom they do matter.

John McGurk of the CIPD was interviewed as part of the background for a white paper published by Lancaster University Management School. The paper was titled 'Learning & Development: Seeking a Renewed Focus?'[33] McGurk said...

> "I am often amazed at how much disconnect there is between an L&D function and what is going on in the organisation design, the change programmes, all of which need to be integrated."

Part of this disconnect is due to the use of specialist language and jargon, which is either not understood by the audience or, perhaps even worse, is misunderstood due to the way that some words are used differently. When you are proposing a solution, make sure you do so in a way that is simple. This is especially important when using a written medium, because you do not have the immediate visual feedback of the puzzled frown.

The Gunning fog index measures the readability of English writing. The index estimates the years of formal education required for someone to understand the text on a first reading. The test was developed by Robert Gunning, an American businessman, in 1952. The fog index is commonly used to confirm that text can be read easily by the intended audience.

There is ongoing debate as to how the fog index should be calculated and what the output means in terms of a required 'reading age'. Nevertheless, it serves to remind us that some text is much easier to read and understand than others.

I put the preceding few paragraphs through a readability calculator at www.readabilityformulas.com and the average result across seven different readability formulas showed a required reading age of 14 to 15 years. You might like to try this for documents and reports that you have written. Of course you must also take into account the included jargon, because this cannot be computed by the readability formulas, which rely on factors such as sentence length, word length and syllable count.

Another simple test for your wonderful proposal for a learning solution is to give it to someone who is ten years old, and ask them what they think it means.

Does the ten year old, at least at a high level, understand from your executive summary what the problem is, what the solution is, and what the ultimate benefits are? If not, I suggest you rewrite it. I am not saying that your audience has the intellectual capacity of a ten year old; I am saying that in order to capture their attention in amongst the flood of information they are exposed to, your document must be very quick and easy to understand.

Does your proposal focus on what's important to your audience, or does it wax lyrical about the things that are important to you? In effect, it is a sales proposal, so get some coaching from good sales people on how they structure their proposals and how they focus on impact and results for the prospective customer.

It's important to realise that, while the 'feel good' aspects of learning and training matter intensely to you, they may not even register with other people in the business. Tell a Finance Director, for example, that the return on investment of your last training intervention was extremely high because 60 per cent of participants said they 'felt more empowered and confident by the end of the two days' and he is likely to roll his eyes in exasperation. When they ask for results, they're not asking about the feedback forms people give you. They want to know the impact on productivity, performance and, ultimately, profits, and they want to know this in terms of measures that they understand.

If your solution is successful, what are the expectations of your key stakeholders, and how will they measure whether those expectations have been met? What language would they use to describe those expectations?

L&D professionals should provide a clear set of expected results to stakeholders. That is really all they are interested in. They really don't care how you achieve the results (well, within reason), but they will be intensely interested in what the expected results are. They want to know if the workers will be able to execute at the point of need. If you spend your meetings discussing the minutiae of what you will have to do to get the job done, your stakeholders will switch off. If, instead, you spend them defining the outcomes of your efforts, your stakeholders will be engaged. Now you're doing something for them that matters.

Susan Meisinger[34], former president and CEO of the Society for Human Resource Management, said that knowing business (finance, marketing and operations) is the ante or ticket of admission. She says...

> "Without this knowledge, HR won't be included in key business discussions where they could provide a point of view, take a position, or challenge an assumption. And, if invited, they won't be asked to stay. Unfortunately, many in HR limit their own opportunities because their expertise is too narrow."

In the book, *What CEOs Expect from Corporate Training*[35], Rothwell, Lindholm and Wallick list the seven competencies that CEOs expect from workplace learning professionals. 'Business knowledge' heads the list.

Improve your business skills and knowledge

A study[36] conducted by the Learning and Performance Institute (UK), found that a knowledge of business skills is something that many L&D professionals currently lack. It asked L&D professionals to assess themselves against the institute's new capability map, which consisted of 27 skills grouped into nine categories. The categories were

1. Live delivery
2. Learning resources
3. Performance improvement

4. Collaborative learning
5. Learning delivery management
6. Analysis and strategy
7. Managing the learning function
8. Business skills and intelligence
9. Learning information management and interpretation.

At the time or writing, over 1,000 people have filled in the survey. Most respondents ranked themselves well for the traditional categories, such as content design and delivery (live delivery and learning resources), but few ranked themselves well for business skills and intelligence.

The report stated...

"Much is made of change today and change is indeed inevitable if we are as a community to avoid being consigned to the 'training ghetto', in which the L&D department does little more than compliance and induction training.

"In order to escape this fate, however, we need to do more than concentrate on expanding our skills in delivery and community/social learning.

"While it is essential to continue to develop these, it is as important, if not more so, to develop skills in those areas of weakness. They are centred on business skills, such as communications and marketing, and unglamorous but essential technical skills, such as competency management, financial management and data interpretation.

"The future of the L&D profession depends on us rising to the challenge of a fast-moving, business-focused environment and developing ourselves in these areas.

"The results suggest that the profession lacks the broader, business-based skills it will need to contribute as part of the organisation of the future. Those leading L&D departments are better skilled than most in these areas, but still lack the breadth of skill required both to lead their departments and to communicate effectively with the rest of the business."

An understanding of business concepts or drivers is not something that is possessed by more than a few working in the area of training, human performance technology (HPT), instructional design (ID), organisational development (OD), and HR, according to Lynn Kearny and Kenneth H Silber, authors of *Organizational Intelligence.*[37]

They found, after running workshops and courses involving 2,000 HR/ training professionals, that fewer than 20 per cent could answer very basic business questions about the organisations for which they worked (either in-house or as consultants), about the strategic issues facing the organisation, and about how they, as L&D, HR or training practitioners, contributed to the organisation's bottom line (or even what the bottom line was or how it was calculated).

Few of those 2,000 people knew where to find documentation about what the business was involved in, its plans and challenges, and how it measured up.

If L&D and HR don't understand key business concepts or the business language of stakeholders, they can't possibly understand the organisation's most pressing concerns and its stakeholders are likely to dismiss their recommendations as naive.

It's difficult to influence decisions or even get the time and attention of the people who make those decisions if you don't have business intelligence, they pointed out. They said...

> "If we don't understand the business concepts and the business language our clients use, how can we understand their most pressing problems? If we make recommendations that do not take the big business issues that clients face into account, how can they trust our recommendations?"

That's why, if you are in HR, L&D or Training, you must understand...

- What opportunities and threats the organisation is facing due to external trends within its own market and the economy; that is, how external systems influence the internal systems
- How growth and profits are achieved by the organisation – you cannot impact the bottom line if you don't know where it comes from
- The organisation's purpose, strategy and goals – you cannot effectively support the journey without knowing the route and the destination

- How the organisation's prospective customers or clients are identified, as well as acquired and retained – all organisations, whether they have a commercial purpose or not, exist to serve customers; if you don't understand how those customers are found, brought on board and kept on board, how can you improve the capability to serve those customers?
- The unique selling proposition (USP) of the organisation's products or services – what it is about the organisation's products or services that make them better than those of competitor organisations
- Why customers choose the organisation's products or services rather than those sold by its competitors
- Why customers choose competitors' products or services rather than those sold by the organisation
- The company's external image and brand – how do customers, potential customers, competitors and other stakeholders perceive your business?
- How the organisation's products or services are created, produced and delivered or distributed – how does the system work?
- How the organisation's infrastructure works.

Go through the above list of bullets and rate yourself on how much you understand. Ask a senior manager in the business for their answers, and see how much your understanding differs from theirs.

Decision makers within the organisation need to be persuaded that L&D and HR bring value and create results that make a difference to the organisation's results. To do that, L&D and HR professionals must learn to

- Communicate more strategically with the organisation's key decision makers
- Communicate what they want and need in a persuasive manner that decision-makers understand
- Reposition L&D and HR as strategic partners rather than service providers
- Use facts, numbers and statistics that matter to the C-suite to strengthen their case
- Communicate the value of the business-level results their initiatives have produced.

L&D veterans Tony Bingham and Tony Jeary[38] say that L&D professionals need a set of communication strategies, skills, techniques and tools that will allow them to shine in the more demanding roles that await them. They say...

> "Those who develop the requisite knowledge, communication skills and business acumen will survive and thrive in the competitive marketplace of the 21st century. Those who don't, won't."

They recommend that L&D/HR professionals develop a deep understanding of their organisations by studying the material that's readily available (for example, annual reports, press releases and articles), interviewing and observing key people within the organisation's hierarchy, and having conversations with colleagues and co-workers.

Doing so will give the L&D professional an understanding of the organisation's business strategies as well as the way information does or does not flow between departments or functions. From that, they will get a better understanding of the organisation's performance gaps.

A systematic investigation will take them a long way towards getting the information they need. For example, L&D professionals need to ask CEOs the following questions:

- How can I help you realise the organisation's strategic objectives?
- What are the biggest human performance problems in our organisation?
- What are the biggest opportunities for improving human performance?
- What one effort could we launch that might have the biggest positive impact on the performance of people in our organisation?
- What do you think my department or team should do to help with the continuing implementation of the effort?
- What should operating managers or supervisors do?
- Are there particular groups of the workforce that are critical to business value? Is there a critical cluster of workers? What do they need to be able to perform better than they are right now?
- What should we do to help make sure that the effort is implemented as intended? That is, what safeguards would be necessary to ensure

that the effort is implemented in the right way to achieve the results
you need?
- What should we do to communicate our successes and our
areas for improvement as the performance improvement effort is
implemented?

Understanding the organisation's vision, strategy and goals as thoroughly as
corporate-level management does is one of the most important jobs for L&D
and HR professionals.

They need to find ways to help the CEO and top level management achieve
their goals, as well as ways performance improvement initiatives can be
used to boost strengths and underpin weaknesses, adding value to the
organisation.

J Craig Mundy[39] writing in the *Harvard Business Review* offers a simple question: "Does it [the contribution of the HR team] cause friction in the business
or does it create flow?" Friction is simply where the actions of the team impede
capability and conversely flow enhances capability and performance.

He suggests that HR teams have become so caught up in the importance of
the role they play (recruitment, benefits, payroll, L&D and so on which offer a
feeling of power to those charged with dispensing them) that they have begun
to think that the business works for them. He goes on to point out that this
is backward thinking. In fact HR and L&D are often far removed from the
process of creating value; instead, they need to focus on ensuring that people
can perform as smoothly, productively and with as little friction as possible.

KPMG's report[40] 'Rethinking Human Resources in a Changing World', is
scathing in its assessment of current HR practices. It says (in reference to the
current global economic environment) "this has required HR to play its part,
largely through making the HR function more efficient, but not necessarily
more effective."

In fact, the report shows that only 17 per cent of businesses felt that HR was
doing a good job of demonstrating strategic value to the business.

The report recommends a complete review of performance management. The
research finds that this is not fit-for-purpose in too many organisations. In

particular, that there's not enough emphasis on what's needed for business performance, and ways that employees and managers can measure themselves against these needs.

It goes on to say...

> "There is often a gap between the ambition and rhetoric of talent management and the practice on the ground. Many talent processes have unfortunately become annual form-filling exercises where business managers comply and HR departments are disappointed with the outcomes."

In closing, the report notes that to improve the profile of HR (or L&D) the function needs to move from administration activities to higher-value activities. It also highlights the importance of involving line managers to a much greater extent and even moots the idea of transferring some of HR's traditional responsibilities to line managers.

The reputation, or 'brand' of HR and L&D is somewhat tarnished. Survey after survey shows that HR and L&D are not highly valued within most organisations because they are not perceived as adding strategic value.

The evidence suggests that in most organisations, HR and L&D simply are not aligned to the organisations they serve. They know that they need to be. They talk about business alignment as though the process were simply a case of repeating; 'we're aligned' often enough, until the rest of the business believes it. Unfortunately, rote repetition does not make something so. The business will not accept that HR and L&D bring something valuable to the table until they see tangible evidence that L&D and HR are more than cosmetically aligned with their needs.

My suggestion is to stop talking about aligning with business goals and start enabling them. Albert Einstein said: "Insanity: doing the same thing over and over again and expecting different results." I don't wish to suggest that L&D and HR are insane, but there is a touch of madness in the 'prescription training' process employed in businesses today. L&D and HR are not unaware of the marginalisation of their contributions, yet they are not making significant progress in addressing the issue of their credibility within the business.

A performance consulting and capability management approach will bridge this gap. It will not be an immediate solution. L&D departments that make an announcement along the lines of 'we're moving away from training and focusing on capability to improve business performance' are unlikely to suddenly find themselves being called upon by the board to demonstrate their prowess.

Gaining credibility is a gradual curve. The focus on capability is an important step in the right direction, but HR and L&D will only begin to be perceived as more credible when they can demonstrate the results demanded by the executive team, and have discussions about the business using the business models that line managers use intuitively.

It is also important that you take time to understand what your 'market' needs. What are the problems experienced around your organisation that you may be able to help with? It is well-known in marketing circles that companies which target their products at the circumstances in which customers find themselves, rather than the customers themselves, are those that can launch predictably successful products. The more fully that L&D understands the challenges that line managers face, the better they will be able to deliver solutions that the organisation values and rewards with continued investment.

The change may take time to work its way up the organisation, but when line managers in departments receive a valuable service they will then begin to champion that service. Senior management will hear that their performance problems are being dealt with effectively and they will come to understand that it is L&D and HR that are driving the solutions to those problems. Eventually, the invitation to the board meetings where the deepest issues are discussed will follow.

Your brand, your credibility

Credibility, and an enhanced brand, arise from the development of skills within L&D and the results provided by L&D. And trust me, the L&D brand is important. You will find it impossible to be effective within your organisation if your brand – that is, the perception that others have of you – is that you are not effective.

The way managers in your organisation approach you gives you a strong indicator of what the brand of L&D is in the organisation. If you are approached by them with a training request, and they clearly expect you to be an order-taker, this tells you a lot about your brand. They are interacting with you in a way that is congruent with what they think you do and who they think you are, in other words, your brand.

Whenever you interact with other parts of the organisation you will be carrying the brand of L&D like a neon sign over your head, and that will encourage people to treat you in line with their perception of that brand. Unless they know you personally very well, they will interact with their mental construct of the brand, particularly when dealing with business issues. The mental construct they have of you and your department is thus a vital part of how they will interact with you, so you need to manage the mental construct they create within their mind.

According to Jeff Bezos, the founder of Amazon, "A brand is what people say about you when you're not in the room". You could take this a step further and say that it is what people feel about you when you're not in the room.

Take a moment right now to reflect on what people would say about you when you're not in the room, and about HR and L&D.

What would you like them to be saying instead?

So much of brand comes down to marketing, in the sense that you need to make visible what you do as well as do it. I highly recommend that you speak to people in your marketing department, or a friend who is in marketing, to discuss how you can rebrand L&D. You might even consider a different name for the department currently known as L&D. What could you call it instead? In fact, when other changes are implemented, a change in name for the department and a change of titles for the team is probably essential.

The perception of your brand, of who you are, and of what you do will be formed whenever there is a touch point with any of your customers. Jan Carlzon called these touch points 'moments of truth'. How you and your colleagues handle those moments of truth is critical to your brand. As your customers walk away from an interaction with you, what thoughts do you want them to have about the quality and success of that interaction?

Start thinking of L&D as a performance consultancy service provider which has customers, and a brand, and therefore a need for sales and marketing activities.

You might even use a basic customer relationship management (CRM) system to keep tabs on your interactions with the different business units.

A basic marketing principle is to find a need within your target market, and then find a way to fulfil that need. Your target market's need is simple: it wants performance in the pursuit of its strategies – which means it wants everyone in the organisation capable of doing what needs to be done to execute the strategy.

It always comes back to execution: doing what needs to be done when it needs to be done. And execution depends on capability as we have defined it. So let's dig a little deeper into exactly what constitutes capability.

Chapter 4

The components of capability

Systems make it possible; but people make it happen.

Kyoshi Suzaki

Capability is a slippery concept. For some time now I have been discussing capability with people in HR and L&D, and with managers and executives in both the public and private sectors. What I have found remarkable is the lack of consistency in how people use the word capability.

Given that any organisation has a purpose – and achieving that purpose is dependent upon the people in the organisation being capable of doing all the tasks that need to be done – I would have thought that capability would be so fundamental to success that people would have a handle on it. Or at least the successful people would.

Perhaps one reason that capability is a slippery concept is that it is actually very complex. A good way to tackle complex concepts is to break them down into components and create some kind of model that we can use. A common way to create a model is to deconstruct what we think of as reality, and remove bits that do not seem relevant until we have a structure that is simple enough for us to understand and make use of.

Of course, this means that the model is not 'true', because it is a subset of reality. It is a representation of a complex system that hopefully allows us to manage that system effectively. So, with the caveat in mind that any model is not 'true', let's deconstruct capability. Let's start by going back to our nice and simple definition of capability. 'Can the worker do the task at the point of work... yes or no?'

If the worker can do the task, all is well and good. If not, or they cannot do it to the required standard, why not? As we look at what stops workers being capable at the point of work, some common themes emerge. That is to say, there are components of capability and each of these components must be at or over a threshold in order for that worker to do that specific task at that specific time.

Some of those components are specific to the person performing the task. They are internal to the performer. And some of those components are specific to the environment that surrounds the performer at the point of work.

If a worker cannot carry out a task you need to look at each of these components and determine which one is preventing the task from being done at that time. And of course, there may well be more than one component below threshold. You are then in a position to start considering how you can remove the barrier(s) to capability, and if the costs of enabling the capability, and therefore the productivity and performance are worth the effort. Will there be an acceptable ROI?

Let's look at each of these components in turn:

1. Knowledge
2. Skills
3. Mindset
4. Physiology
5. Environment.

But before we do that, it is worth pointing out that none of these components is truly independent of the others. They all interact as a system. The reason we separate them is to better understand the system, and although we can work on the components separately, we must never lose sight of the fact that they are interdependent, and a change in one is likely to change some of the others.

To help explain these components in context, I want to introduce Susan. Susan is a barista in a local coffee shop. Why a barista? I have found that many current learning and development thought leaders are obsessed with the 'knowledge worker' to the exclusion of everything else. There is no doubt that the knowledge worker plays an important part in the efficiency of British business, but the stark truth is that 57 per cent of the British population consider themselves to be 'working class'.[41]

The National Readership Survey of 2006 showed that blue collar workers make up a minimum of 36.9 per cent of the workforce (categories C2 and D) and there is no doubt that a large number of blue collar workers are likely to fall into the 29 per cent of the workforce in Category C1, which alludes to a more skilled area of work, but which in reality includes many more highly-skilled blue collar workers.[42]

In effect, blue collar workers make up a large percentage of the workforce. In a discussion I had recently with a large supermarket chain, they said that well over half of their employees did not have a work email address. Workers like Susan are not an endangered species; in fact, they still make up the majority of workers in the world today.

Knowledge

To know what you know and what you do not know, that is true knowledge.
Confucius

Knowledge consists of facts, figures, information and data that the worker needs to know prior to tackling the task in hand. This internal memorised knowledge is the primary outcome for most formal training and people are subjected to exams and tests to try and measure how much of it they have. Alexander Pope's classic essay points to the need for full knowledge in order to be capable.

When looking at the knowledge required to do a task, consider whether that knowledge needs to be available from memory or whether the knowledge could be sourced from the environment. For example, knowing what road signs mean is knowledge required for driving. I use the example of knowledge of road signs because I gained a personal experience of the importance of this when I first started driving in the UK. In the UK, the 'no entry' sign is a round red circle with a horizontal white line in the middle of it. In New Zealand where I grew up and learned to drive, the no entry sign looks quite different. I found this out one evening in London when I was stopped by one of those uniformed gentleman with flashing blue lights. I was driving the wrong way down a one-way street which luckily was devoid of any other traffic at the time. My New Zealand accent must have been somewhat more pronounced back then, and I escaped with a verbal warning and a rather pointed lesson in what a 'no entry' sign looks like in the UK.

Unlike knowledge of the different road signs, knowing how much air to put in the tyres is knowledge which could be looked up each time it is required. This kind of 'external' knowledge falls under the fifth component of capability, which is environment.

As another example let's consider how knowledge effects Susan, our barista. The modern coffee shop is far removed from those of my youth; back then your choice was simply coffee or no coffee with milk and sugar as optional extras. Today's global business environment has seen the offerings of a coffee shop multiply exponentially. There are different types of bean to choose from, different serving methods, different types of milk and sugar and even different syrups to add to my coffee. It's no longer possible to say 'A cup of coffee please'; instead you ask for 'A skinny Brazilian latte with hazelnut and brown sugar'.

Susan's job would once have been a simple order-taking process in which coffee was poured into a cup and handed over. Now, she needs to know about coffee and all the alternatives her customers might desire.

Some coffee shops will have an incredible range of coffees, from hard-hitting high-caffeine Italian roasts, to delicate Guatemalan flavours, right through to Kopi Luwak – that bizarre bean which has been neatly processed through the intestines of an Indonesian civet cat before being harvested for roasting and drinking.

When a customer arrives in Susan's coffee shop, it's her job to guide them through the weird and wonderful world of coffee. She needs to be able to ascertain their taste preferences and point them in the direction of the perfect bean to help them with their choice.

She needs to be able to describe the flavours and aromas and put them into a context that the customer can understand. In short she needs in-depth knowledge of coffee beans.

This is the first step in the process; she now needs to be able to explain the differences in the way the coffee is produced. Does the customer want an espresso, a latte, a cappuccino, for example? She needs to be able to concisely explain what's involved in each cup.

Susan should also be able to walk the customer through the types of milk available to them and why soy may be the right choice for the lactose intolerant. She should know which production will best suit the strong natural taste of brown sugar and which is better served with syrup, honey or processed white sugar.

Finally, she should be able to advise on additional flavours. How will a splash of raspberry affect the average latte? Will it render it a taste sensation or turn it into an undrinkable concoction, leaving the customer unhappy at parting with their money?

At first glance, it appears that a barista needs very little knowledge. After all, their job is to make you a cup of coffee – how hard can that be? Yet when you start to dig into Susan's world you find that product knowledge is a cornerstone of her work. To be a great barista Susan needs a wide-ranging understanding of coffee.

Susan began to learn about coffee the day she became a barista and she continues to learn as new blends are invented and new ideas are tried and tested within her workplace.

In most businesses the provision of knowledge is seen as the responsibility of the learning and development function. When a new employee starts, they are often given some form of induction training. In the case of a new barista, it might be a one-day course covering a range of information, including lots of interesting coffee facts and trivia.

One of the unfortunate things about memorised knowledge is that it decays over time if it is not used. A worker who has sufficient knowledge today to do a task may well fail to do that task in six months' time if they have not had to recall or use that knowledge in the intervening period.

Hermann Ebbinghaus, a German psychologist, conducted a series of experiments on memory. His 1885 paper, 'Memory: A Contribution to Experimental Psychology'[43] gives us an insight into how much we forget over time. His research showed that we unlearn or forget nearly half of what we learn within a few days of learning it. A lot of research has been done since then that confirms the idea that we are poor at retaining memorised knowledge. In a training context, we typically forget around 90 per cent of the course content within one month.

The research also shows that the more often we are exposed to information, the less likely we are to forget it, and we know this to be true from our own personal experience. Think back to an old job you had a few years ago. Tasks you could do with ease back them may well be difficult or impossible for you now because you have not been using the knowledge required to do the tasks.

The organisation which relies on training alone for the knowledge component that leads to capability is setting itself up to fail. This degradation of knowledge has a significant impact on how an organisation should manage the knowledge acquisition process. For example, an induction process for a new employee would probably be more effective in the form of a learning pathway that takes place over a period of time rather than presenting the information in a training course.

The other problem is that knowledge that we have memorised goes out of date. It decays, and has a 'use-by' date. The answer, surprisingly, is not to know more, but to know less and use technology to store and find the information when it is needed. The balance between 'know it' information and 'find it' information has changed rapidly over the last few decades.

Robert Kelley of Carnegie Mellon University has been asking people for over 20 years "what percentage of the knowledge you need to do your job is stored in your own mind?" In 1986, the answer was about 75 per cent, but by 1997 the percentage had dropped to between 15 and 20 per cent. When Kelley ran the research again in 2006, the percentage had dropped again to between eight and ten per cent. Although these figures are bound to vary greatly depending on the job role being considered, there is a clear trend that people are needing less and less memorised knowledge to do their jobs effectively, provided they have access to the knowledge they need from tools and technology in their environment.

Skills

Knowledge is not skill. Knowledge plus 10,000 times is skill.

Shinichi Suzuki

For our purposes here, we can consider a skill as some behaviour that requires practice in order to be done well. All jobs require many skills, such as walking, reading, typing and driving. For most jobs, we can add in social and communication skills, and also specific skills, such as mental arithmetic, driving a JCB digger or mixing cocktails with a flourish. The range of skills required is huge and each one only comes with practice. A certain amount of practice is possible within a formal training environment, but most skills that are specific to a job are learned and developed on the job. This is what Shinichi Suzuki demonstrated in his years as one of the world's most renowned music teachers: practice equals skill and there is no innate shortcut to those skills.

When I was a student, I worked during the summer holidays as a forklift driver in a frozen goods warehouse. During the day the temperature in the warehouse would slowly rise to about -10°C as warm moist air managed to get in past the hanging plastic strip curtains whenever we drove our forklifts through them. Overnight, with the big chillers on full blast, the temperature would plummet to -35°C and the moisture in the air would precipitate out as snow. One of the first jobs every morning was sweeping the snow out of the aisles between the long lines of pallet racks.

Over the years that the warehouse had been in operation, a layer of ice had built up on the floor so that walking around the warehouse and driving forklifts was quite challenging, and it required quite a lot of practice to develop the skill to do so safely. One particular skill I had to learn was how to use the ice in order to skid-turn a forklift to face the racking in an aisle, when the width of the aisle was narrower than it would be in a normal warehouse. By making the aisles narrower, they were able to fit extra racks into the warehouse, but this meant that the only way to load or unload the racks was to pirouette the forklift like an ice skater on the ice.

Unfortunately, skills also deteriorate over time. This is why pilots keep doing refresher courses in simulators to experience emergency and unusual flight conditions. And that is also why I probably couldn't drive a forklift on ice if I tried it again today.

The next time you're in a coffee shop, watch the baristas in action. Note the speed at which they move, and even the grace of those movements. They are economical and clearly well-practised. You could not hope to match their skill without many hours of practice. Watch also how they juggle half a dozen orders from different customers all at the same time.

Especially watch for someone who is clearly new behind the counter. How would you know that they are new? It would be apparent from their lesser skills in handling their tasks compared to their more experienced colleagues, and this difference would be visible in their behaviour.

In addition to the obvious motor skills that a barista needs in order to be proficient at their job, there are other skills that will only come with practice. These could include, for example, the ability to quality-check coffee based on visual and olfactory clues, and even clues from the noises that the coffee machine makes. They would also need skills in communicating with customers, especially in circumstances where the customer is angry or complaining about something.

Traditional training departments would build a course for new baristas. They would ensure that before Susan starts her customer-facing duties she has had a chance to learn to use the machines. They will provide an environment in which she can practice her new skills and achieve some form of competence. They may even certify Susan competent as a barista at the end of this training program. After all, if Susan can demonstrate at the training that she can make the perfect cup of coffee, she should be able to do so in all environments, right?

Unfortunately this is not the case. The model of competence, first developed by Noel Burch[44] of the Gordon Training Institute back in the 1970s tells us why this is not so.

We begin the skill-learning cycle at a point of unconscious incompetence (or unskilled) where we simply don't know what we don't know. Before Susan decided to become a barista, she would have been completely unaware of the intricate demands of the job and she probably didn't give them much thought.

When she took up her job, Susan became consciously incompetent. She now knew that she needed to be able to do certain things to make a great cup of coffee, but she didn't know how to do them. Then the training team arrived and after Susan's training they pronounced her consciously competent in the art of coffee preparation.

Conscious competence is simply knowing that you can do something, and being able to do it. However, Susan is probably not consciously competent for very long before she slips back into conscious incompetence; she forgets some of what she learned in the classroom and loses the skills she practised. She can no longer produce a quality product on demand.

Fortunately, most coffee shops do not employ a single barista and the trainee can be supported on the job by someone else with proven skill. The move to conscious competence will occur, but probably not as early in the employee's career as the training team would like to believe.

This support is a crucial factor in learning skills and one that is often neglected by the 'on demand' training team. A course is delivered. The trainee is seen in a controlled test environment to be competent in their skills. They get a certificate and the training team moves onto their next course delivery. Fortunately, in many instances the workplace naturally provides additional support – as is the case at Susan's coffee shop. It is, however, worth bearing in mind that other employees – for example, those in unique roles without other colleagues to rely on – may well need a formal program of support to become consciously and then unconsciously competent.

Over time, Susan may become unconsciously competent. If she carries out a task to a high standard daily, she will no longer think about how she roasts the beans, she'll just get on with it.

Things are rarely this simple. It is likely that, while Susan has to carry out some tasks on a near daily basis, other tasks are likely to be carried out much more infrequently. The Kopi Luwak coffee I mentioned earlier is extremely expensive. The definitive Kopi Luwak requires a farmer in Indonesia to roam the coffee plantations looking for the droppings of a civet cat. He must then retrieve the beans from these droppings and collect them until he has enough to sell.

A cup of Kopi Luwak is often more than £10 in a coffee shop. Given that most of us can't spend that much money on a cup of coffee every day, it is often seen as a bit of a 'gimmick', designed to show that the shop has a genuine knowledge of coffee rather than to be sold to customers. However, given that it is available, sooner or later someone will order it.

By the time someone asks Susan for a cup of Kopi Luwak it may be weeks or months since the shop last sold a cup. Is it likely that Susan will remember perfectly how to prepare this coffee? In this instance she remains consciously incompetent.

Then there is the alternative scenario, in which Susan slowly begins to diverge from unconscious competence. She makes small changes in her routine and these become part of her 'autopilot' approach to preparing coffee. Over a longer period of time, it is likely that some of the changes she introduces are going to reduce her ability to make good coffee. Here, she has become unconsciously incompetent again. She doesn't realise that she's introduced such a change and thus doesn't know how to correct it.

This model of learning is one that we are all familiar with to some degree. Performance organisations are always looking to steer skill development so that it remains in the sweet spot of 'unconscious competence' without it falling back into any form of incompetence.

Mindset

People often say that motivation doesn't last. Well, neither does bathing. That's why we recommend it daily.

Zig Ziglar

Mindset includes things such as motivation, confidence, self-esteem, attitude, commitment, courage, tenacity and even duty and responsibility. The foundation that sits under many of these is engagement, and we have all seen the research reports on how important engagement is. There is a proven direct correlation between high employee engagement and organisational success. We know this intuitively from our own experience, and all the research confirms it.

When we are talking about mindset in terms of a capability component, we are not talking directly about engagement. We are talking about the more transient aspects of mindset or attitude, including motivation. Motivation to do a task in the moment is quite fluid. If a worker has had an argument at home, they may well feel less inclined to work today, even though they are normally well motivated. Conversely, if a sales person receives a good sales order, their demeanour changes and they approach their next sales calls with renewed spirit and motivation. This variation in motivation nonetheless sits on a foundation of engagement, or disengagement, which tends to be more stable.

Mindset is somewhat at the mercy of the other factors affecting capability. If any of them are below the threshold – and thus the task is hard or impossible to do – it will put a damper on mindset. Conversely, if all the other capability components are above the threshold, then the job is easy, and even fun, to do. Results are easier to achieve, and things like motivation and confidence will inevitably rise. If mindset is consistently good, it leads to better engagement.

Because of this, it is usually better to tackle other components of capability first, and you may well find that if there is a mindset problem it will automatically disappear when the other components of capability are brought up to threshold. The bonus is that the underlying engagement is also likely to improve even though you have not been directly running an 'engagement' programme.

Let's return to Susan in the coffee shop. It was her birthday yesterday and because she is a young, sociable person she had a wild party to celebrate. She went out on the town and had more than a few drinks with her friends. She danced until the early morning hours at a local nightclub before returning home to grab a couple of hours sleep before she came to work.

At work Susan has, to put it mildly, a bit of a hangover. She's tired because she didn't get a full night's sleep. Would you think that Susan was a 'fully motivated employee' today? No, I don't think so either. Notice that this lack of motivation is not affected by the benefits that have been put in place at her workplace to help drive engagement. Such benefits might include flexible working, recognition in the workplace, non-cash rewards or incentives, paid parental leave and time for study. The typical tools of engagement programmes are not enough to offset the potential short-term swings in mindset.

Now, if you're thinking that this is a contrived example, because Susan did this to herself, let's look at another situation.

The coffee shop is busy. There's a huge queue of lunchtime customers wanting their daily caffeine fix and needing to return to work once they've had it. The coffee machine is broken. It's a mechanical failure and it's beyond Susan's skills to repair. The shop has called for an engineer, but the earliest they can be there to start work is two hours away.

It's Susan's job to explain to the customers that they can't have their favourite fancy coffee today. They'll have to settle for a cup of tea or a glass of milk for the moment. How do you think Susan's motivation will hold up as each customer expresses their outrage or frustration to her? It is likely that as the time goes by she'll feel more and more frustrated about bearing the brunt of her customers' ire and that will impact on her usual sunny disposition and level of customer care.

It is also possible for motivation to increase from other factors. In our coffee shop, it's now Christmas Eve and when Susan came to work she was a little bit down-in-the-dumps about spending Christmas Eve away from her family. However, each person in the queue so far has been a regular customer and each of them has given Susan a fairly substantial tip for Christmas. In fact, in the first hour on duty Susan has made nearly £100 in tips! Now, there's a spring in her step. She is more than her normal cheerful self; she feels like she's walking on air. Susan's motivation has shot up into the stratosphere. She is having a great day!

One of the things that will affect engagement scores is the frequency of episodes at work that either frustrate or delight workers, and therefore affect their mindset in the moment. Adding corporate benefits and making workplaces nicer places to be is important, but the feelings that are regularly experienced at work also have a major impact on engagement.

Who hasn't had that moment of frustration when a computer, a machine, a printer or something has packed up and left us unable to be productive? Who hasn't found their motivation slipping at such a point? If this happens often enough, it will definitely reduce engagement.

In fact, I would argue that capability is at the heart of engagement and that if someone feels capable of doing a job it becomes easier to do and thus more fun. A natural consequence of enabling capability is engaged employees, provided they are doing meaningful work.

One of the things I find astounding is the number of engagement programmes that are run at great cost by organisations that attempt to boost engagement while doing nothing to mitigate the factors that disengage people in the workplace. These disengaging factors are easy enough to find by asking two questions in the following order.

1. What frustrates you on a daily basis?
2. What do you tolerate now that used to frustrate you?

Most people, even the ones who are very engaged at work, will be able to answer those questions with a list of things. Just take a moment now, and think how you would answer those two questions in your current job.

The vast majority of people would like to do a good job at work. When they start a new job their engagement level is usually incredibly high. They do not turn up wanting to do a bad job. Their natural state is engaged. It is only when they encounter things at work that frustrate them, that annoy them, that contravene their values, that they become disengaged. Very often they become disengaged in response to how they are treated by those who have some control or authority over them – their leaders, managers and supervisors. Disengagement occurs when a person's needs, in terms of security, social interactions, self-esteem and self-fulfilment, are not met.

Much of what disengages people at work is the same stuff that stops them doing their job, that stops them being capable. So first address the disengagement factors: look at how to enable people and ensure they are capable of doing the task at the point of work. When you have done that, your investment in engagement programmes and other corporate benefits will start paying off handsomely.

Physiology

There are many jobs that require certain physical characteristics, such as strength, or height, or manual dexterity. This is not about being able-bodied or disabled. As a species we have a huge variability in our physiques, our motor responses and our intellectual capacity.

Although it might seem politically correct to say that anyone could do any task, we all know this isn't so. Only some of us would be able to carry bricks on a building site all day long. Only some of us have the IQ that is required to handle actuarial mathematics, and only some of us have the physical appearance that is required of a fashion model.

Susan's job is physically demanding. In order to do her work, she needs to be on her feet for most of the day. She moves from machine to machine, carries stock back and forth and so on. Without a certain level of physical fitness, Susan would simply be incapable of doing her job.

When I worked in the frozen goods warehouse as a forklift operator, there were seven forklifts, and two of them were models which had quite low safety frames. As I am much taller than average, I was unable to drive these two forklifts for a full shift due to the fact that my head was bent over to fit inside the safety cage. My physiology rendered me incapable of driving those two forklifts.

Physiology is not concerned with the differences between the disabled and the able-bodied. It is simply a statement of capability. If your physiology is not up to the task you are required to do; it is going to be nearly impossible for the work to get done. Performance is always a result of capability. Someone who is physiologically incapable of doing a job cannot perform.

It's important to recognise that physiology does not just apply to physical factors. While it is true that if you want to be an astronaut, for example, you will need to be superbly physically fit to even be considered for the role, you will also need to be intellectually capable of doing the job to make the shortlist. In general, an astronaut is expected to be qualified to post-graduate level in a science. Not all of us have the aptitude to reach graduate level in the sciences and fewer still have the aptitude to take this to a post-graduate level.

Many learning and development functions appear to believe that anyone can learn anything, even though this is clearly untrue. Perhaps it is politically correct to think so, but investing in trying to overcome physiology is misguided, even if the intentions are good.

There is a great quote by Robert Heinlen, the science fiction writer: "Never try to teach a pig to sing; it wastes your time and it annoys the pig".

There are only two sensible options for addressing physiological capability in the workplace. The first is at the recruitment phase. A job should have a defined set of characteristics required to perform it well. However these physiological characteristics are defined, they should be tested during the recruitment phase and candidates that do not have them should be eliminated before hiring.

The second option is one that you are legally obliged to consider for the disabled and one which you may wish to consider for candidates who are exceptional in all other respects but a single aspect of physiology. This option is modifying the workplace to accommodate the physiological deficit. Changing the workplace cannot overcome every physiological issue, but it can address many of the most common ones, such as a worker being unusually tall (or indeed unusually short) or somewhat overweight (or underweight).

In the case of the disabled candidate, if you can reasonably overcome the physiological issue through modifying the workplace, you should do so if they are otherwise the best candidate for the job. In other instances, you should see if there is a business case for adapting the workplace for a well-placed candidate.

Environment

You can't teach people everything they need to know. The best you can do is position them where they can find what they need to know when they need to know it.
Seymour Papert

Notice that the previous four components of capability are all 'attached' to the worker. The fifth component, environment, is independent of the worker. Think of the environment as anything around the worker that affects their ability to do the job in front of them, at the point of work.

The first four factors will vary from worker to worker. Some will be more knowledgeable or more skilful than their colleagues, others will have better attitudes compared to their peers and some may be better suited physiologically to their work than their co-workers are. The environmental aspect of capability is often constant to the entire team of workers. This means that changes to the environment can often enable entire groups of workers, so they are now capable of performing, or disable them, so they cannot perform.

If Susan's coffee machine is broken then she cannot make coffee, and nor can her colleagues. The failure of a coffee machine renders Susan incapable of doing her job.

Let's go back to the example at the start of the book of the mechanic who was unable to repair the car due to the unavailability of a spare part. He was not capable of doing the job because there was something missing in his environment. Other things that might have stopped him repairing the car could have been the absence of a special tool, an electronic diagnostics machine that did not work with that model of car, or that the spare parts store was locked and the foreman had taken the key with him on his lunch break.

Another possibility is that what you need to do the task is available, but difficult to get. In fact, it might be so difficult to get that your level of motivation to do the task is not sufficient to drive you to break down the barriers between you and what you need to do the task. So, we also need to consider the barriers between the worker and what they need to access in order to be capable of doing a task.

By the way, this is one reason why leadership is successful in improving performance. Powerful leadership develops high levels of motivation so that people will break down the barriers and obstacles within their environment that would otherwise stop them doing their job. The bigger the barriers in your workplace to capability and therefore performance, the better your leaders need to be in order to develop sufficient motivation for people to overcome those barriers.

Another approach is to remove the barriers rather than try and improve your leaders. Surely removing the brick from in front of the wheel of the car is easier, and cheaper, than trying to push the car over the brick.

One way to find those barriers is to ask people first what frustrates them about their job, and then what it is that they are tolerating about their job that used to frustrate them. It could be something as simple as the way they have to login to access the intranet, or even that the font used for the intranet is too small. You won't know until you ask.

Think back over the last week of doing your job and notice how many tasks you were unable to do, or found difficult to do through no fault of your own. In other words, you were competent and motivated to do the task, but something outside of you, that is, something in your environment, stopped you from getting the task done or made it extremely difficult to do.

Now consider the employees in your organisation, or workers in general. From time to time they will be rendered incapable of doing the job in front of them at the point of work, and this lack of capability is considered a performance problem. What proportion of those performance problems would be due to factors related to the employee, and what proportion would be due to factors in their environment?

In my own experience, and as I have discovered in many conversations about capability and performance, the environment is responsible for well over half, and in some cases almost all, of the performance problems. Given that the environmental factors that affect capability are most unlikely to be solvable using training, it starts to become obvious that training should not automatically be seen as the solution to any performance problem.

Later in the book we will look at a detailed process to determine which capability factors are contributing to a performance problem. Many of them will be environmental factors. For now, let's consider a few of them, to give you some examples of the factors that might be involved.

Performance support

Marc J. Rosenberg, in his paper *At the Moment of Need*[45], defines performance support as a "tool or other resource, from print to technology supported, which provides just the right amount of task guidance, support, and productivity benefits to the user – precisely at the moment of need."

What job aids and information can the worker call upon in the moment of need? How easy is it to do this? Is the performance support truly embedded into the workflow? Is the information accurate, relevant and practical? Is it layered appropriately?

Gary Wise in his blog 'Feeding the Performance Zone with EPS'[46] describes the layers that could be included within an Electronic Performance Support (EPS) system.

"Building an EPS solution requires that we first decide what 'opportunities' should be on the menu of choices that may include:

- Contextual Guidance – in the form of a role-oriented map of a workflow… a 'You are here' kind of visual, or a Chinese menu with selections from column A and column B.
- Step-By-Step Instructions – a sequential 'how to' guide of quick steps designed for quick, in-and-out usage… a 'Drive-Thru' or a 'To Go' approach to feeding the need.
- Deeper Detail – when quick steps are not enough and the task is complex enough to warrant additional information to better guide the Performer.

- Brokered References – where additional content like company policies, methods, technical specs, etc. are required to complete the task and are stored in another URL-addressable repository.
- Structured Learning – where the Performer may choose to gain access to courses/modules in the LMS or access an application playground to practice working through simulation exercises.
- Social/Collaborative – assets or opportunities that require live conversations or messaging with SMEs, project team members, content owners, and/or Help Desk staff.

"The number and combination of choices included in an EPS solution are a function of what Performer task requirements exist, and how to best serve the Performers' moments of need. Factor in 'urgency' to resolving the need, and/or 'risk' and options less time-sensitive may better serve the need. For example, accessing the LMS for a structured learning course on Fire Safety is likely not the best choice when one's hair is on fire."

This layering of performance support is important in order not to overwhelm the performer with information greater than their immediate need to succeed at their task at the point or work. It is important to avoid the temptation to just give them the whole user manual.

We live and work in an information-intensive world. Someone coined the term 'infobese'. New knowledge is growing exponentially, but the half-life of knowledge is decreasing dramatically. We must know more, but what we know has a shorter shelf life than ever. There is a fast-growing need to inject this current knowledge at the point of work where it is applied, and now, with technology, we can.

Accessing information these days is as easy as lifting a finger. We have an expectation that we can access information at any time, and according to a study done at Columbia University[47], this expectation results in lower rates of recall of the information itself and enhanced recall instead for where to access it. The Internet has become a primary form of external or transactive memory, where information is stored collectively outside ourselves.

In Susan's coffee shop, when she got back from her initial training, she was fortunate enough to have many performance support tools available when she needed them. For example, there was a chart attached to the side of the coffee machine which showed the controls and how to use them. The chart, which included pictures and flow diagrams, reminded Susan of the safety chart in the pocket of her airline seat last time she went on holiday. She also knew where the user manual for the coffee machine was kept so that if she needed more detail on a rarely-used setting that was not on the chart, she could find out. She was grateful for the chart so that she didn't have to wade through that huge user manual to find information on basic and common operations.

Tools, software

Does the worker have access to the right tools to do the job? Is their computer fast enough and loaded with the right software?

Susan's team doesn't just make coffee, they also work the cash register. In keeping with the current trend, their cash register is in fact a computer with an automated tray for holding the money. The computer is as old as the branch she works in. When it was installed, it was the latest model and it did the job admirably. Over time, the software on it has been upgraded over and over again, while the hardware has been left to stagnate.

It used to take a couple of seconds to ring up a customer's order, take the money and give change. Now it takes much longer. Every time Susan or one of her colleagues rings up the order the computer seems to need time to think before it finally compiles a total and lets Susan enter the amount the customer is paying. This is a mild inconvenience when the shop is quiet, but a major frustration when there is a queue of impatient customers.

Spare parts and other resources

Can the worker easily access the kinds of resources they need for their job, for example a meeting room, or even an organisational resource, such as the accounts department?

Susan has been working for her employer for a couple of years now and they've been impressed with her work. In fact they're so impressed that they've decided that Susan can now take over from the training team, so instead of sending new baristas to head office to learn the basics of their trade, they can learn in their own environment instead.

This sounds like a great idea. Susan is extremely competent as a barista. She's a warm, friendly and patient person, who can clearly explain what is needed on the job and when. She can bring her experience of working with customers to the table and bring a great deal of relevance to the initial training program. It's also less expensive for the company to deliver induction training this way. Susan benefits from increased responsibility too, and this may be the first step on the ladder to management if she does it well.

A month later, the initial review of this activity is not so enthusiastic. The review shows that the trainees don't seem to know what they're supposed to do. They don't have the knowledge or skills that they would be expected to have at this stage of employment. At first glance it appears that Susan is a terrible trainer and that the training activity will have to return to head office.

Fortunately for Susan, the training team isn't made up of order-takers and they dispatch someone to the branch to determine why things should be so out of line with their expectations.

What they discover is that there's no suitable place in which Susan can offer training. The only room which is suitable for a quiet chat is the manager's office and the manager is permanently occupying it to ensure that the business is administered properly. Susan has been forced to train on the coffee shop floor, cramped onto the smallest table (so that customers are not put out by her activity). The noise level for much of the day makes it impossible for her student to take in what she's saying. The training is becoming increasingly disjointed because the lack of private space means that Susan is being dragged into helping out when things get a little busy.

Systems and processes

Does a mandated procedure stop people doing what they need to do to get the job done? Or slow them down so much that they lose the desire to do it?

Susan, like all of us, has the right to a request paid holiday from her coffee shop post. This could be a very simple process, but unfortunately in her company it is not.

At the moment Susan has to fill in a holiday form and have it signed by her supervisor. This must then be passed on to the store manager for their approval too. The store manager then needs to send the form to the area manager for their sign off. Then the area manager passes the form onto HR for their agreement. Once the form has been circulated like this it is then returned to Susan's store manager to check once more before she is allowed to go on holiday.

The process is so over-complicated and time-consuming that nobody in the chain enjoys working with holiday requests. They get pushed to the bottom of the pile again and again. What should be a simple case of someone asking for holiday that they are entitled to and then taking that holiday has become a battle of organisational control. Susan hates asking for holiday, particularly for short one- or two-day breaks, because the process can mean that she loses out on cheap hotels, flights and so on while she waits for approval.

When this holiday approval process was designed, it was done with great care. The idea was that each department or individual affected by Susan's holiday would have some input into the decision of granting her request. Sadly, it simply doesn't work.

Incentives

Are any incentive or bonus schemes aiding or hindering the work? Some incentive schemes cause unhealthy competition which can lead to lack of collaboration.

Susan's company had announced a new incentive scheme. The barista who made the most sales in their region during the month of December would get an all-expenses-paid trip to the United States. They'd get to visit Florida and New York and take in theme parks and shopping experiences that would normally be too expensive for someone like Susan to afford. Susan knows she's good at her job and she knows how to upsell her customers, so she's keen to start selling so that she can start planning her vacation.

Incentive schemes like this are common. The principle behind them is sound. If you want your workers to sell more, you provide them with an incentive to do so. They sell more and everyone wins. Right?

The incentive scheme drawn up at the Head Office level looks good on paper. Which barista would turn down a free trip to America with all their spending money and so on thrown in? Susan's certainly excited about the potential. The trouble is that many incentive schemes don't operate as planned. Let's look at what happened in the coffee shop.

Susan wasn't the only person to be excited by the promotion. All of her colleagues were too. A trip to America is a considerable incentive. The problem was that there was only one prize to be won. In order for Susan to win, she not only needed to beat colleagues in other stores – she also needed to beat her colleagues in her store.

As the results came in it became increasingly clear that Susan was dropping behind in sales. She found herself being outmanoeuvred by her other colleagues who wanted to spend more time at the till (ringing up those sales) and less time making coffee (which the incentive scheme failed to reward). Susan's frustration came to a boiling point when one of her colleagues physically pushed her out of the way at the till in order to ring up a high-value sale.

They had an argument about this in front of the bemused customer. Every customer in the store could overhear the gist of the argument and many of them quickly made for the exits. Susan's manager was appalled. His team has always worked well together; they like each other, and support each other. The new incentive scheme had set them against each other and, worse, it was costing his store business.

This is all too common in the workplace. Bonus and incentive schemes need to be designed to ensure that the overall productivity of all workers rises. When a scheme is designed to find a single winner it all too often produces far too many losers and the company itself is the biggest loser of them all.

Feedback on what is required

Do the workers get sufficient feedback on what they are doing well and what could be done differently?

Susan's manager is a nice chap. He really is, but he tends to stay in his office doing his reports, ordering supplies and generally focusing on all the administrative tasks that keep the coffee shop running smoothly. Provided there are no arguments or customer complaints, he does not really get involved with the customers. Susan has had to figure out for herself what constitutes a good job as she has had little guidance from the manager.

Culture

How does the culture impact upon capability? Is it a 'can-do' culture, or one where people wait to be told what to do?

Susan had to deal with an unhappy customer today. The customer had found a fly in her drink and complained. Susan immediately swapped the drink and upgraded it to a larger size in an effort to keep the customer happy. The new manager was incensed by this. In her previous company, upgrading a beverage to respond to a complaint could only be authorised by a manager. Otherwise it would be considered stealing.

Culture, or the 'way we do things around here', has a massive, and often almost invisible impact on capability. It is invisible because it is so pervasive, so much a part of the background environment, that people do not notice when cultural factors are driving behaviour.

Management style and effectiveness

How well is the worker managed? This is probably one of the biggest factors of all to have an impact on capability, because it is the manager who is responsible for the worker's environment, skills practice, mindset and, to some extent, knowledge.

In order for Susan to serve her customers well, she in turn needs a service from her manager to provide her with a number of things that enable and empower her. Thinking of management as a service which the manager provides to their team is a fundamental break from the old command-and-control style of management. This 'management as a service' concept can be quite challenging for many managers, especially when they realise that the arbiter of the quality of any service is the service recipient.

Thinking of management as a service was popularised by Jan Carlzon, the CEO of Scandinavian Airline System (SAS) between 1981 and 1994. He visually represented this by turning the traditional hierarchy pyramid upside down with himself at the bottom and the customer-facing people at the top. His impact on SAS was nothing short of miraculous, as it went from one of the lowest-rated airlines in Europe, and losing money, to being voted airline of the year three years later and making good profits. He wrote a book called *Tear the Pyramids Down,* which was translated into English and published under the title *Moments of Truth*. The American Management Association, in the 75th anniversary issue of their magazine in 1998, called this one of the most important developments in management of the 20th century.

An article in Forbes magazine[48] shows that bad management has an extraordinary range of effects on employee wellbeing. The stress caused by poor management can make workers ill – that's literally ill rather than figuratively. Stress leaves us open to colds, strokes, flu, disease and even coronary problems. Stress is also something that people take with them into the rest of their lives. If someone is miserable at work, it's likely they're sharing that misery with their family, friends and colleagues and creating more stress.

The Forbes article suggests that bad management practices cost the US economy over $350 billion a year. Another article in the Telegraph[49] offers the figure of £19 billion a year in losses to the British economy, just from time off taken by unhappy staff. Bad management is expensive.

Others

There will be many more factors within the environment that could disrupt the capability of a worker, and many will be unique to specific jobs. Very often it is only the people who are actually doing the job at the point of work who can identify the factors.

The key thing to remember is that the environment is a very much larger part of capability than it might appear at first glance.

Chapter 5

Performance consultancy process

*My greatest strength as a consultant is to be ignorant
and ask a few questions.*

Peter Drucker

A consultant is a professional who provides expert advice in a particular area or specialised field. In our case the field is performance, specifically the performance of an employee while doing their job.

The origins of the word consultant go back to the Latin word 'consultare' which means 'to discuss'.

It is defined by Gerald Weinberg[50] as "the art of influencing people at their request". He says "people want some sort of change – or fear some sort of change – so they seek consulting in one form or another."

Few people request help when their world is working for them and behaving rationally from their perspective. It is when things go wrong that they need some kind of external assistance to help them get their world working again.

They do not know how to fix their world because, from their perspective, it is now behaving irrationally in a complex and confusing way. Without help, they are liable to try various solutions in the hopes of fixing their world, but there is every chance those solutions will not work, and may even increase the confusion and complexity. It is almost as though the irrationality they see around them infects them as well. You may have noticed, for instance, how frequently someone who asks for advice will then attack angrily because they don't like the requested advice.

Sometimes help is solicited explicitly; sometimes we can sense the need for it though the request remains implicit, and sometimes we sense that others need help even when they do not recognise it themselves. It takes a lot of courage to ask for help, so people often don't ask, and yet anyone looking in from the outside can see that they need help.

When someone needs help and asks for it, a difficult dynamic is set up between the helper and the client, because the helper is automatically invited to adopt an expert role. The implication is that the helper has something that the client is lacking. On the other hand, once an effective helping relationship with the client has been developed, the client and consultant together can diagnose the situation and develop appropriate remedies.

The ability to build and maintain a helping relationship is central to any form of consultancy, including performance consultancy. One way to think of this relationship in your mind is to imagine the client saying 'I need you. I cannot say so directly, so please find a way to help me without destroying my sense of worth'.

Ideally, of course, the start to building an effective consultancy relationship begins with an explicit request for consultancy help. However, as we have seen in the previous chapters, this is unlikely to happen given the current attitudes towards L&D. A request for help will indeed happen, but it will have a multitude of strings attached and be couched in the form of a request for specific services, typically training. In effect, what has happened is that the problem has been defined retrospectively in terms of a solution that the problem holder thinks they understand. They are grasping for something familiar in amongst their confusion.

This means that the first stage of any performance consultancy process is always to steer the relationship into a place where genuine consultancy activity can occur. You need to disentangle the solution from the problem. The consultation process itself can then proceed through a set of diagnostic steps that will ultimately lead to actions and changes that will improve the situation for the client. The real problem with designing change is not designing the change itself, but correctly identifying the problem the change is intended to solve.

The performance consultancy process is designed to step the problem holder back from their problem in order for them to see it clearly, and therefore have a better understanding of the kind of solution that is required. It is essential that the client and the consultant work together jointly on the diagnostic steps so that the client can see the problem for themselves. This is important because the process is itself an intervention, and at all times the client, or problem holder, must own the problem and be responsible for decisions made regarding interventions and solutions.

Everything you do as a performance consultant is an intervention in the client's world. There is no such thing as pure diagnosis. How the diagnosis is done has consequences for the client's system. The common description in many consulting models of a diagnostic stage, followed by recommended prescriptions, totally ignores the reality that if the diagnosis involves any contact with the client's system, the intervention process has already begun.

An effective process will also ensure that the client learns to use the diagnostics tools and process for themselves so that in the future they will be better equipped to deal with the complexities of performance, and their world will not seem quite so irrational.

A client who understands the tools in the process, and who makes decisions to implement solutions based on what comes out of the process, is far less likely to try and slide the problem from their desk onto yours. It is not the consultant's job to take the client's problems onto their own shoulders. The reality is that the client has to live with the consequences of the problem and the solution, and so the client must retain ownership of the problem and the solution.

This also means the client may well take kudos and claim responsibility for the success of the interventions you collaborated to create. This is okay. Even if the client claims the superhero role, everyone knows how vital the trusty sidekick is to the process of winning. Others will seek you out so that you can also help them win.

The consultancy relationship

Many cultures emphasise self-reliance and put a value on solving one's own problems. For a person to seek help and make themselves temporarily dependent on another person is a de facto confession of weakness or failure, particularly in Western, competitive, individualistic societies. Indeed, some people may consider that seeking help is tantamount to admitting that they cannot do their own job. At the beginning of a consultancy relationship, the two parties are in a tilted or imbalanced relationship.

There is a natural inclination on the part of the client to redress the imbalance, or even gain the upper hand. This can explain why they are sometimes insistent on doing things a certain way and using their choice of solution. This gives them a sense of control over the situation. They may seek to use their positional power, or network power (friends in high places) to force you, the consultant, into a process of their choosing. They may say they don't actually have a problem, provided you do what they are asking you to do. The secret here is to go with the flow, but in such a way that you steer the flow towards a consultancy relationship which will allow you to actually be a consultant. You need a relationship that equilibrates the status between the client and the consultant. The detailed steps to doing this are in the next chapter.

One of the things to avoid doing in a consultancy relationship is 'running ahead' of the client. You may recognise key factors, causes and solutions far earlier than the client can see them. Remember that you have an external perspective and more familiarity with the process, and they are still burdened with the complex irrationality of their problem. They will probably take longer to see the important parts of the puzzle.

It is better not to share these early insights, because until the client has come to the same realisation, they may well be defensive and unwilling to listen to what you have to say. And of course, another possibility is that you might be wrong. If you jump to conclusions that are incorrect, you will damage your credibility, and therefore your 'brand' as a consultant.

Another interesting, and frustrating, aspect of consultancy which I have experienced many times myself, is that what you regard as a brilliant insight is hardly noticed, and some throwaway comment or question results in a turning point for the client that changes everything. I remember coaching a very senior person in a large bank many years ago on some aspects of his performance that were limiting him in progressing to the next level. Several years later I met him at a networking event. He had indeed managed to get his promotion and thanked me for helping him make that step. When I asked him what was the difference that made the difference, he said it was a comment I had made when we were having lunch after a coaching session, and we were not in 'coaching mode'. This is why it is important to focus on the process, and the discussion this generates, rather than the consultant as the superhero who will save the day.

How does it all start?

If the business says they have a performance issue, either current or anticipated, what do they mean by that?

Basically the business wants something to happen, but it's not happening.

A performance issue arises when someone is not doing what they are tasked with doing, or something is not doing what it is supposed to do. And if it is something not doing what it's supposed to do, chances are in its history there was someone who made a bad decision, which meant that in time the thing was unable to perform. They made a decision about setting it up which meant that at some point in the future it became incapable.

Pretty much any performance issues can be traced back to people, to actions or inaction, or to decisions that turned out to be wrong. This is why it is so easy to point the finger of blame for poor performance directly at the performers. If someone is not doing what they are supposed to do, and you are wielding a big enough stick to ensure that they want to do it, then it must be because they can't do it, and therefore they need to be told how.

It is this kind of reasoning that explains why managers reach out for training as the solution to their performance problems. So, of course, they look around them for someone to supply some training. You need to be aware that operations people still think of you as 'training', even if you have some fancy title like people development. You have training rooms, and training IT suites, and if they want training they have to come to you. When you talk to them, you still mostly talk about doing training. Of course they think of you as the training department, whatever your name.

Ron Drew Stone in his book *Aligning Training for Results*[51] talks about the training request being driven by a one or more of a combination of six business situations. He refers to these as the six signals:

1. Business deficiency – an opportunity exists to improve the business due to a deficiency in one or more business outcome measures.
2. Execution deficiency – employees are not executing an existing job requirement or task as they should.
3. New expectation – new knowledge, skills, competencies or behaviours are required to perform a new or existing job or task.
4. Business change – change occurs in business or operational philosophy, policy, process, procedure, product, strategy, technology or service.
5. Business opportunity – current performance is not necessarily a problem, but an opportunity exists to provide training, development or other interventions that will sustain the organisation's performance or avoid negative consequences in the near future.
6. Business compliance – a need exists due to a management directive or a regulatory, licensing, accreditation or certification requirement.

In their mind they need training, so that is what they want, and that is what they ask for. At this point, you have some options. You can acquiesce to the request for training, and deliver it as requested. You can refuse the request on the basis that they are incompetent to decide what training is needed by their team, and they should send their people on the standardised training programme that everybody gets. Or you can use a performance consultancy process to develop a detailed understanding of the root causes of the perfor-mance problem, and create some solutions that are likely to work better than the requested training.

Gary Wise drew the parallel between a performance problem and an airliner crash in his blog 'Finding the Learning & Performance Black Box'.[52]

> "Question: If flawed performance was a jet airliner with a broken engine how far would it fly?
> Answer: All the way to the scene of the crash.

"And the scene of the crash is precisely where Training should show up to investigate the potential for building learning and performance solutions... after they find the black box.

"The point of impact is where the NTSB searches for clues. The first thing they look for is the Black Box because it maps every action taken, word spoken, and mechanical function that transpired on the way to the crash. They accomplish rigorous discovery by interrogating the black box to determine root causes. Without root causes how can they recommend remedies to prevent future crashes?

"To assume pilots need to be trained on how not to crash, may completely miss the mark and waste big bucks on unnecessary interventions. Instead, they pursue thorough investigative data-gathering to isolate what went wrong in order to determine the actual cause(s). That is an exacting discipline that has a rigorous protocol of discovery. We [Training] need to follow that example and apply our own rigorous discovery protocol when we receive a training request caused by [*allegedly*] poor performance.

"Truthfully, we will never know what is required until we investigate root causes at the scene of the *crash*... or the explosion... or the muffed sale... or the key account lost... or the material waste created... or the law suit. To put it another way, how many training programs have we invested precious dollars only to find out we have not moved the performance needle a whit? Been there; done that. Yes, I've been guilty of training to fix symptoms myself. We all have at one time or another by being obedient, responsive order-takers from stakeholders convinced they have a training issue."

The real problem at this stage is not so much the performance problem itself, but the lack of understanding of what is causing that poor performance, and the knee-jerk reaction to apply training as the solution. The problem owner wants a solution, but in the vast majority of cases, what they want and what they need are different.

Just because you want something, this does not mean that you need it. Just because you need something, this does not mean that you want it. Read that sentence again and think about that for a moment. It is the root cause of much suffering in this world, and it has a large part to play in failed training programmes.

We 'buy' what we want based on emotional drivers rather than the rational drivers of need. We often end up buying things that felt good to buy at the time because that's what we wanted at the time, only to find out later that we didn't really need them, and we didn't get the results that we were seeking. However, when someone buys what they want and it is also what they actually need, they do get the results they were seeking because their wants and needs are aligned.

When a manager asks for training, it is almost certain that their wants and needs are not aligned. That is, they are asking for what they want, but it is most unlikely that it is actually what they need. The performance consultancy process outlined here is designed to help them understand what they actually need, and that understanding will in itself realign what they want. Once they can see what they need, that will become what they want, and they will let go of their original ideas about what they thought they wanted. A primary outcome of the process is to assist the problem owner align their wants to their actual needs.

One way to think of this is that every problem has boundaries that define it. The problem holder is inside the boundaries with the problem. It is like being inside a box, and all you can see is the inside of the box. Unfortunately, the solutions to the problem are all outside the box. Luckily our problem box has transparent walls when seen from the outside, so your goal is to enable the problem holder to move outside the boundaries of the problem so they can look back at it from a place rich with solutions.

The process

The performance consultancy process itself can be divided into three stages.

Stage 1. Getting the meeting

Initially the problem holder just wants to throw their problem over the fence at you, so they feel like they have done something about it, and they can move onto other things. They will not want to spend much time talking to you about it, and this presents a problem, because you cannot be effective as a performance consultant during a corridor conversation. Stage one of the process is selling them on the idea that they need to meet with you.

The primary outcome of this first stage is to convince the problem holder that they need to spend some time with you in a face-to-face meeting, and get that meeting scheduled sooner rather than later.

Stage 2. The meeting

Given that you were successful in the first stage, you are now in a meeting with the problem holder. They may well still be somewhat sceptical about the need for a meeting and are begrudging the time they have given you for it. There is a step-by-step process detailed in chapter 7 that explains how you deal with this scepticism, and how you progress from there.

The primary outcome of this second stage is to align the wants of the problem holder with their actual needs. And of course to do this, you need to help them go through a diagnosis process to find out what those actual needs are.

Stage 3. After the meeting

If the meeting has gone well, you will now be collaborating together on solving the performance problem. It is likely that more information will need to be gathered from the performers, and more stakeholders will need to become involved in order to deliver the range of solutions that are probably now on the table.

The primary outcomes of this third stage are to complete the diagnostics, agree the solutions to be used, and start taking action. In effect, the performance consultancy process will morph into a project management process.

The performance consultancy process is a sequence. Sometimes you will have to loop back to iterate a specific step, but this is the pathway to follow to get you to a very definite end result. When you have run this sequence a few times with people, you will be able to start losing some of the steps because your 'clients' will already know how the process works and perhaps they have already done some of the steps on their own before you even get together. It gets easier as you gain experience with it and as the people you are working with gain experience of your approach and the process.

There will be some uncertainties when you start using the process because you will be behaving differently to what people expect. As they come to value the results that emerge from the new way you are doing things, they will treat you like a valued partner rather than an order taker. There is a learning curve on both sides of the fence for both you and your internal customers.

As you get more skilled and knowledgeable about how the sequence works and, more importantly, why it works, then feel free to change and adapt it to suit your own circumstances. In the beginning though, run with the sequence as it is described in the next three chapters.

People sometimes ask, why should L&D get involved with this kind of detailed performance diagnosis? Shouldn't this be the managers' responsibility?

It's a fair point and, ultimately, yes, it should be the manager's responsibility. However, they have come to you asking for training in a way that shows they really have not thought through their performance problem in sufficient detail. In effect, their attempt at diagnosis and solution has failed. It is almost certain that if you deliver what they are asking for in terms of training, they will not get the improvement in performance and results that they seek, and it is again almost certain that they will then blame the training or how it is delivered for the lack of results.

So when someone in the business comes to the learning department and asks for training, it is akin to a poisoned chalice. Indeed, the first sips of wine can taste good, even from a poisoned chalice. You are being asked for something that you know how to do and you enjoy doing, and it is good to feel wanted. You get to help people learn stuff, and after all, isn't that why you are there? The request for the training may even come with some budget attached which gives you some sense of job security.

The problem with the chalice is that the poison will, in time, cause you problems. Every training course that fails to live up to expectations, even unrealistic ones, damages the brand of L&D, which will become more and more marginalised. If you want to be in the driver's seat, and I assume you do, you cannot continue to simply take orders for training at face value, and continue to drink from the poisoned chalice.

Donald H Taylor[53], Chairman of the Learning and Performance Institute, goes so far as to say that parts of the business will start actually doing their own people development, and bypassing L&D altogether except for generic and compliance training. L&D then ends up in the Training Ghetto. He says...

"L&D is seen as being about training delivery, in the classroom or online, and nothing else. The Training Ghetto is where good information goes to die. It's the training department that's in the basement or the Portakabin across the car park. It's the cost centre that gets cut when times are hard, and which is reluctantly retained for compliance and induction training. It isn't seen as contributing to the business and the good people there are usually promoted out. Nobody wants to stay in the ghetto."

If you want to avoid, or even break out of the training ghetto, then becoming a performance consultant is your best bet.

It is also much better for the business if L&D starts focusing on performance rather than learning. For reasons we have already discussed, most other people around the business will automatically default to requesting training and, as we know, training may well not be the answer. Given it is the focal point for training requests, L&D is the obvious place to introduce a reality check on every request.

The benefits

In addition to helping you sidestep the poisoned chalice, using a performance consultancy approach will give you, and your organisation, a number of other benefits.

- You will improve the brand of L&D because you will get better results for the business.
- Your focus on what's important to the business rather than just on training or learning will be welcomed by line managers.
- You will get involved in a wider range of activities than just doing training in the pursuit of performance.
- You will become valued by the business as an expert in your area and with expertise that is essential for business success.
- There will be a clear line of sight between your activities and business performance.
- You will be invited into projects and programmes in their early stages, rather than as an afterthought.
- In time, you will be invited to a seat at the top table because they want you there for your expertise.
- You will be in a position to easily justify budgets for learning programmes which you judge to be essential.

- You will have the means to be able to prioritise the many requests that get placed on L&D.
- And... you will avoid the training ghetto.

One of the benefits that people who are using a performance consultancy process often refer to is the change in the quality of the relationship between L&D and the rest of the organisation. This can make a profound difference to how much enjoyment a learning professional can get from their job.

Chapter 6

Stage 1 – Getting the meeting

The greatest good you can do for another is not just to share your riches, but to reveal to him his own.

Benjamin Disraeli

The primary outcome of this first stage is to convince the problem holder that they need to spend some time with you in a face-to-face meeting, and get that meeting scheduled sooner rather than later.

Stage 1 starts with 'the request' for training, when they

- Stop you in the corridor
- Send you an email
- Leave you a voicemail
- Pop in on the way to another meeting
- Send you a requisition form
- Have their PA call you
- Say they already have budget
- Say they only have a few minutes

- Say they have agreed it with other people
- Say they have already found an external supplier
- Specify which training course they want.

They do not define their performance problem in any detail, and there is an expectation in their approach that you will acquiesce, and deliver the training programme or other learning intervention they are asking for, based on the minimal information they have provided.

It is probable that the problem they are seeking a solution for is causing them some significant stress, and they just want to get it off their plate and onto someone else's. Asking for training to solve the problem is a way for them to shunt the problem sideways so they can feel that they are doing something about it. I'm not saying that the request for training is a flippant or insincere request. The problem is likely to have been growing for a while and they will have put some thought into how to solve the problem, so when they come asking for training solution, they do genuinely believe this is a good solution. They are also likely to be impatient now that they have decided on a solution.

When they come to you with a training solution requirement, they are very attached to their solution in their mind. You need to honour that attachment and the fact that it is their solution, their baby. By the time they approach you, they will have convinced themselves that training will indeed be the magic bullet. That means the conversation, at least initially, needs to revolve around tweaking and configuring their solution so that it gets the results they want. The performance consultancy process, as outlined here, will take them from that starting point to where they need to be.

I hate the 'L&D challenge' that some people talk about. I'm certainly not the first to talk about the potential problems in simply acquiescing to training requests from other parts of the business. I have seen many articles and blogs where people recommend that the response to a training request is to robustly challenge the need for it. In effect, they are recommending that the response to a training request is to say 'you are probably wrong'. In my opinion, there is no need for this kind of confrontational response.

It is far more important to gain and keep rapport, and join them in their reality rather than challenge it. You are then in a position to lead them from their reality to a better one and do so in such a way that they are quite happy to walk with you on that journey.

In order for you to do that, you need to get some quality time with them, so your focus during this first stage is to get the meeting that will provide that quality time. In a culture where meetings are frequent and called for any reason whatsoever, this may be relatively easy. However, the person making the training request will be busy, and probably unwilling to invest further time on a problem which they now think they have given to you.

Your task now is to 'sell' them on the idea that a meeting is required, which means that you must come up with some good enough reasons for them to want to invest their valuable time in that meeting.

In order to make this 'sale' you will need to have a brief conversation with them. If they have stopped you in a corridor to place the order of the training, you are already in conversation. If they have left you some kind of message, then you will need to go to their office or waylay them in the corridor to make your sale.

In a nutshell, your approach should be like this:

1. Acknowledge the request for training or other learning solution
2. State that you need some more detail to ensure that what you deliver is customised to suit their exact needs
3. Ask for a brief description of the problem
4. Ask what it would cost the organisation if the problem is not addressed
5. State that given what they have just told you, it is essential that you get together with them in a meeting to discuss it in more detail so you can design an effective solution
6. Arrange the meeting.

Let's look at this approach in a bit more detail.

It is important that you let them know that they have come to the right place. In whatever words you want to use, congratulate them on the wisdom that led them to knock on your door. By now you will know what they are asking for, whether that is a one-day training on financial jargon or a five-day management training. Repeat back to them what they have asked for and say that it is certainly the kind of thing that you would be able to do for them.

Your next gambit is to suggest to them that their situation is probably unique in some way and it is doubtful that any of the 'off-the-peg' solutions will work well enough to solve their problem. Whatever you do for them will need to be customised especially for them, and therefore it would be very helpful to have a brief description of the problem they are experiencing that the training will fix.

As they describe the problem, it is important that you empathise with their plight. If the problem is causing them significant stress, they may well need to vent their frustration on a sympathetic ear. They may also be reticent about giving you the details of the problem because that will expose their part in allowing it to happen. They may well feel threatened in terms of their credibility just because they are admitting that they have a problem that they need help with. Be patient, and listen to build trust and rapport. You will learn a lot about them, about the problem, and about what they expect from you.

Take notes, even if you don't need to. This is a simple way for you to acknowledge that what they are saying is important. Even if you're on the phone, stop, and say 'wait a minute, I'm just writing that down'.

Notice that the presupposition within all of this is that you will actually deliver the learning intervention they are asking for, but that you need more information.

The next thing you need to do is ask about what would happen in terms of financial loss if nothing is done about the problem. A few people who are data oriented may well be able to answer this, because they have crunched through some numbers, but they will be in the minority. Your goal at this stage is not so much to get an exact figure, but to make it explicit that there is a real cost to the organisation if this problem is not handled effectively, and the implicit subtext of this is that this cost will be blamed on them as the problem owner.

If they ask why you need a 'cost of inaction' figure, say that you need to get a sense of the scale and urgency of the problem in relation to other things that you are being asked for by other people. Just like anybody else, you have a need to prioritise and manage your budget and resources. This statement of scarcity is common in many sales pitches. How many times have you been told that today is your last chance to get this deal, or there are only ten left in stock so hurry up and buy now?

If they can give you a figure, even if it is just a guess, accept it at face value unless you think it is far too low given what they have already said about the problem. If you think it is too low, say something like 'that surprises me. I would have thought the figure would have been much higher because of ..., but you know your department better than I do'. Whether they agree with you or not, you have raised the possibly unwelcome thought that they have underestimated the problem.

If they cannot give you a figure at all, and say it's impossible to estimate, they are just ducking the issue. In order for this to be a significant problem to them and the organisation, it must have some kind of cost implication. Ask them for a gut feel of what the figure could be. You could use words such as 'Would the cost be £10,000 per year, or £100,000, or £1 million per year?' You will probably get a response like 'Well, it is definitely not £1 million per year, but it is certainly costing us more than £10,000.' There is a good chance they may well then give you a figure, because in order to make that statement they must have a figure in their mind. You can also use a phrase such as 'I know that it's not easy to come up with a cost figure for this particular problem, but if you had to hazard a guess, what would that guess be?'

Let's assume that we have a rough guesstimate of £75,000. This figure can now be used as a lever to help sell them on the fact that you both need a meeting to discuss this further. At this stage, the higher the figure, the better it is for you and your outcome of getting a meeting, so you might ask further questions, such as 'Is this temporarily or seasonal?' or 'How will this affect the product promotion we are doing this autumn?' Given the nature of the problem as stated, you may be able to think of implications outside the immediate area of responsibility of the problem holder that actually make the potential cost for this problem far bigger than they realise.

This is where you put on your 'this is going to cost you a lot' face, like the repairman who has just investigated a problem in your heating system. You can even do the traditional sharp intake of breath and suck your teeth in surprise at what you're about to say.

'That's not a trivial amount of money, and that's only a guess so it could be a lot more than that. We both need to get this right, because getting it wrong and letting these mounting costs continue will not look good for either of us. On the other hand, if we can get this right we will be saluted as heroes. To get it right, we had better make very sure that I understand the problem in sufficient detail to customise a learning solution that will be effective. Let's schedule a meeting next week for an hour to properly look at the detail.'

Now, if they don't want to get together for an hour to talk about a £75,000 problem in order to solve it, that is kind of weird. I'm sure they regularly have meetings where the value decisions are far less than what this problem is costing.

If they still resist a meeting, you can say that you simply do not have enough detail to customise the training to fit their exact needs, and if they want their problem solved you've got to have that detail to make the training work. Stress that you want to get it right for them so you need the detail. There is no shortcut available in order to produce an effective solution. The subtext of this is that if they care about solving the problem, then they will meet with you. In a sense, this is a challenge, and how you handle it will depend on your relationship with the problem holder, and the political landscape. The number of people who will flatly refuse an hour-long meeting to discuss the problem, and continue to insist that you just deliver what they have asked for, will be very, very small.

An alternative, of course, would be for them to delegate that next meeting to somebody else on their team. This is not ideal, but still far better than just taking the order for the training.

Set a time for the meeting, and then send them a brief outline agenda which would state that you will be looking at:

1. The problem
2. What it is costing the organisation
3. What the desired outcome is in terms of changed behaviours.

You could add to the agenda a statement that the during the meeting you want to run them through some questions since you have to get the details you need to design a solution that is cost-effective and will produce the results that everyone wants. You want to set the frame of the meeting in such a manner that they think it will be an easy meeting for them to participate in. Again, this is not about challenge, it is about helping and collaborating.

Hopefully, the agenda gets them thinking so they are a bit better prepared to engage with detail about the problem when you do meet. They may even have crunched some numbers to come up with a more accurate and defensible figure on the costs of the problem. Notice that on the agenda we have mentioned behaviour, and what success will look like. Chances are they have not previously considered these in any detail, and so you need to give them some notice that you will want to discuss them. There will be other items on your personal agenda, but for the moment they are your secret.

You will need an hour for that first meeting and there will likely be further meetings to follow-on, but you don't talk about them yet. Right now you are just focused on your primary outcome of this first stage, which is getting that first meeting. I have yet to figure out any other ways of doing this without a meeting. To take them through this process effectively, you need to be face-to-face, especially with someone you don't know well.

They could choose to bring a colleague with them to the meeting, but I would recommend that it is kept low key, with no more than three or at most four people, including yourself. Do not let the first meeting get out of hand with lots of people.

If they have come to you with a problem, but without a selected solution, that is absolutely fine; you still use exactly the same process. In fact, it is preferable if they are approaching you to help them find a solution rather than trying to mandate 'their' solution as a fait accompli. If they come to you without a predetermined solution, then they are looking for your help and the sale of the meeting is simple, because that's really what they want anyway.

Chapter 7

Stage 2 – What to do in the meeting

Managers who are skilled communicators may also be good at covering up real problems.

Chris Argyris

The primary outcome of this second stage is to align the wants of the problem holder with their actual needs. And of course to do this, you need to help them go through a diagnosis process to find out what those actual needs are.

This way, you will gain clarity for all parties, and loosen the attachment the problem holder has to their initial chosen solution. This meeting will open the mind of the problem holder to the possibility that training might not be the only or perfect solution, and other parts of the organisation may need to get involved to help solve their performance problem.

Of course, if the diagnostics process confirms that training is indeed the best solution, then at least you move into the training room with a lot more information about what is required from the training, and how you can measure its success.

The problem holder may attend the meeting with an attitude that varies from begrudging the time because they think the decisions have already been made, through to curiosity in terms of what other information might be driven out by this 'process' that you have mentioned. As you change your brand, and as you are seen to be providing an effective consultancy process, they will come more and more to collaborate with you rather than feel they are under duress. This is a sign of your success in changing your L&D brand.

Occasionally, the problem holder will attend the meeting with the intent to use their positional power or manipulation skills to get you to do what they want. One reason for this might be that they have already stated their decision about a solution to their boss, and now feel they have to stand by that commitment. They have therefore decided not to brook any interference with the solution they have asked for in order not to lose face, and will refuse to 'play your game'. Nigel Harrison has written an excellent small book *How to Deal with Power and Manipulation*[54] when acting as a performance consultant in an L&D role. It includes lots of good general advice on handling the consultancy relationship and also some specific advice on how to handle the 'power players'.

Make sure that you keep an eye on the time during the meeting, because you have a lot to do. Focus on the primary outcome of the meeting rather than on getting each step of the following process completely finished. Several of the steps are very open-ended, so it is a judgement call on your part as to how far you pursue them before moving onto the next step. Do not get bogged down with detail and then have to rush things at the end, because you are then unlikely to get what you want out of the meeting. I would highly recommend that before you run this process for the first time, you do a dry run with a colleague to test how long the different steps might take for you, and find out where you have some uncertainty about how to conduct the process.

The problem

The first thing to do in the meeting is ask the problem holder to restate the problem. Problems seldom stand still so there is every likelihood that it has changed in some way, even if that change is only in their mind because they have thought about it following your previous conversation. In anticipation of this meeting, they may also have gathered further evidence about the problem and discovered that it is bigger, or smaller, or growing, or even spilling over into other areas.

Use your active listening skills. Try to assume as little as possible about the problem. Check your understanding of any jargon they use. Your attitude should be one of curiosity about the problem, and how it impacts the wider system. Reflect back what has been said to you to reassure them that you are paying close attention, and that you are understanding what they are saying. Take notes, even if this is not what you would do normally; note-taking acknowledges the importance of what is being said. Also make sure you acknowledge the way they feel about the problem, because it is how they feel that will be having the most impact on them. If the problem is causing them a great deal of stress on a day-to-day basis, they may take the opportunity to vent their frustrations, so a sympathetic ear will help you with rapport.

As well as listening, you need to prompt and question to take the conversation where you need it to go. Questioning is an art in itself. The right questions can make challenging an assumption easy; the wrong questions can be seen as a declaration of war. No-one likes to feel that their understanding and authority over a situation is being undermined. Supportive questioning will develop trust and confidence in the L&D practitioner, and over time the questioning can become more direct as this confidence develops.

In, *Tools for Teaching*[55], Barbara Davis offers the following types of questions for use in the classroom and they can be equally effective when challenging assumptions in the workplace.

- Exploratory questions: these allow you to gain understanding of the basic facts and knowledge in place; 'what is...?' These lay the ground work, not for challenging an assumption, but for understanding the problem through the eyes of the manager facing it.
- Gentle challenges can be offered in a way that presents a greater quest for understanding the problem; 'how do you explain...?'
- You can dig a little deeper into an issue by asking comparison questions. Asking a manager to compare one situation to another may allow them to think more clearly about the details of what's involved.

- When you wish to examine the motivation involved in a decision you can ask 'why?' People often fail to consider problems in depth. A surface level of understanding does not yield the true source of incapability. Asking 'why?' over and over again allows the manager to become granular in their understanding of a problem.
- Action questions enable the manager to determine a course of action which seems appropriate; 'what should...?'
- Examination of these actions can then be done with 'if..., then what...?' cause and effect questioning.
- You can also broaden the examination of an issue; asking 'what else...?' can help with this.
- A particular hypothesis or assumption can be delicately challenged by asking 'what if...?'
- Issues can be sorted according to priority with the simple use of 'what is the most important...?'
- Finally, it can be of benefit to both parties to ask summary questions to sum up what's been agreed and what's been discovered; 'what is your understanding of what we've agreed?'

By the way, although 'Why?' is a very powerful question, be careful in its use. It may push the problem holder onto the defensive as they justify their actions or seek to avoid blame for the problem. Rather than 'Why did you choose that course of action?' use the question 'what were you hoping to achieve by doing that course of action?'

The behaviour gap

As they talk about the problem, guide the conversation towards the current behaviours that are part of the problem. At the heart of the problem, there will be people who are doing the wrong things, or not doing the right things. Make sure the problem holder is clear about what is actually happening at the moment and, in particular, focus on behaviour. It is surprising how often they know there is a problem because some downstream measures or outcomes are not as required, but they actually have little hard evidence or understanding of what people are doing that is causing that problem.

You have to tackle this a little differently if the performance problem is one that is anticipated because of some future change, rather than a current performance issue. You can still run the same process with a future problem, but I suggest you stick to current performance problems until you get a better understanding of the end-to-end performance consultancy process.

Once you have a common understanding and description of the current situation, and current behaviours, start focusing on what the problem holder wants to happen instead.

There is a pretty good chance that they will not be able to give you a good set of success criteria and they cannot in detail describe a future where the problem has been solved. This is particularly true if the predominant motivation pattern is 'away from', because it focuses them on what they don't want rather than what they want instead. It's a kind of 'anywhere is better than here' response to their problem. They just know that they have an itch they have to scratch. They won't have thought through the details of desired behaviours or outputs. They are just hoping that the training they have asked for will remove the pain.

Some questions you can ask that will help the problem holder define what they want are:

- What do you want instead?
- What do you want people to stop?
- What do you want people to start?
- What are they doing now that works and you want them to continue?
- What needs to change?
- What is the ideal alternative?
- What would you want people to do more of?
- What needs to happen faster?
- What needs to happen slower?
- What is not being completed properly?
- How would you know that people are doing the right things?
- How could you measure a successful change?
- What will you see, hear or feel when the problem has been solved?
- Who else will notice when the problem is solved?
- How will they know the problem has been solved?
- What will the numbers and measures look like when the problem has been solved?

Within your questions, keep a positive frame on things. For example, the question 'When this gets fixed how will you know?' includes the presupposition that the problem will be fixed. This is better than using 'If this problem gets fixed, how will you know?' which leaves room for doubt about a successful outcome.

It is also worth doing a simple visualisation exercise with them by saying 'Just stop for a moment, and clear your mind, and imagine you are 12 months out in the future. The problem is solved and things are going well. What do you see, hear or feel?'

Get really detailed about the desired behaviours. Here is an example from a call centre that sells cruise holidays. They were seeking improvements in the number of add-on packages that were sold alongside each cruise. An add-on package could be something like a wine package, a spa package or a theatre package, where payment upfront would guarantee a better price for the services than the passengers could obtain once they were on the cruise. The behaviour they wanted was that the add-on packages were mentioned to the new customer just after they had purchased a cruise. It was soon realised that this behaviour description was not detailed enough. How did they mention the packages? In what order did they mention them? What tone of voice did they use, apologetic or excited? At what stage in the sales process did they do it, and how did they word it? How did they upsell from one package onto the next? A relatively complex set of behaviours is required in order to effectively carry out the upsell of the add-on packages.

The more detail you have in your desired behavioural state, the easier it is to measure this, because it is more observable in a quantitative way. It also encourages people to buy into helping with the solutions, because they have a much more specific endgame to go for. You might like to think about wrapping the SMART goal-setting qualities around your desired behavioural state.

You absolutely must get a handle on what success looks like to the problem owner at a detailed level, and you must have enough notes so that you can write this down as the agreed desired outcome. What are their 'conditions of satisfaction'?

You may have already realised that if you have gone through the above steps and have a defined outcome with some success criteria, and a detailed set of future behaviours that will be in play when the problem has been solved, you have actually set up your measurement criteria for Kirkpatrick levels 3 and 4.

Here is a reminder of the four Kirkpatrick levels taken from the book, *Kirkpatrick Then and Now: A Strong Foundation for the Future*[56].

Level 4: Results

The degree to which targeted outcomes occur, as a result of the learning event(s) and subsequent reinforcement

Level 3: Behaviour

The degree to which participants apply what they have learned during training when they are back on the job

Level 2: Learning

The degree to which participants acquire the intended knowledge, skills, and attitudes based on their participation in the learning event

Level 1: Reaction

The degree to which participants react favourably to the learning event

It should be noted, however, that there is considerable debate around the relevance of the Kirkpatrick model to informal or blended learning, where the intervention is not centred on a specific learning event.

The value of success

If you are like every other L&D department I have ever spoken with, you have a limited budget and resources. You will need to prioritise the projects that you commit to doing, and the only justifiable way to decide which ones to do first is to consider their value to the business.

It is therefore essential that the problem holder produces some defensible figures that will show the value of a successful project in dealing with their stated problem. They may squirm in discomfort at having to do this, either because they consider it difficult and unnecessary, or perhaps even because they don't know where to start in terms of getting some figures pulled together. They should be comfortable with the concept of a case for a project involving the day-to-day business of the organisation, but in all probability they have never had to do that for a learning project.

They need to understand that L&D resources are limited, and they are in effect bidding for those resources, based on the size of their problem and the anticipated ROI. You also need this information in order to fend off other managers who try and jump the queue with smaller problems, particularly if those other managers are more senior and are trying to use their positional power, rather than a sound business case, to jump the queue.

Other stakeholders

It is likely that, as you get more detailed about the output behaviours you want, other stakeholders join the picture, because parts of those behaviours may depend on the activity, input or systems controlled by others. The cruise package upsell is an example where sales and marketing will need to be involved, because the way the sales agents mention the packages needs to be consistent with what's on the website and the brochures. It also needs to be worded in an appropriately enticing way – one that shows that the add-on packages are good value for money and it's worth buying them on the phone, rather than trying to buy them later, on the cruise.

At this stage, it is a very worthwhile spending a few minutes to pull together a stakeholder map/diagram to determine who is involved. This will add further clarity and will almost certainly trigger further thoughts about what is going on right now, and what the desired outcome will look like.

A stakeholder map offers a way to visualise the interconnections between the various stakeholders and the problem. On a large piece of paper or a whiteboard, put a small circle in the middle; this represents the problem. Now draw other circles on the map to represent the people or groups of people who are affected by, or affect the problem, linking these to the central circle with lines. You can add further detail by using the length of the line from the central 'problem' circle to each stakeholder circle to show the magnitude of the affect, so that the stakeholders shown nearest the edge of the diagram are only peripherally involved. You can add arrows to the lines to show the direction of the effect. You can add colours, such as red and green, to show if the effect is positive or negative. Feel free to add any other embellishments that help you and the problem holder to visualise the way the problem is actually part of a larger system. You may also come across types of stakeholder diagrams called 'rainbow' or 'onion' diagrams. By all means use these if they suit your needs.

People are often surprised at the impact their performance problem can have on other parts of the business, even if that impact has so far not been noticed.

- Would other departments also incur costs if the problem is not solved and does this add to the urgency of solving the problem?
- Who else has a stake in the successful solution to the problem, and would their view of what success looks like be different?
- Is the problem causing any internal or external relationship issues amongst the different stakeholders?
- Is there a wider underlying cause that affects other departments, even if they have not yet realised it?
- Has the problem been imported from another department, so that actually the solution must be put in place over there if you are to deal with the cause rather than the symptom?

It is often the case that, once some kind of stakeholder, system or network diagram is drawn up, understanding of the problem increases, because many problems occur in the interface between different divisions, silos or teams.

Something else that happens when you draw a stakeholder diagram is that it starts to become apparent that other teams and departments will need to be consulted. They are likely to have a different perspective on what success looks like and they would therefore define some of the success criteria and success behaviours differently, because they will focus on the aspects of behaviour that matter to them and directly impact on their own interests.

Barriers

At the centre of your stakeholder diagram will be the group of people who are currently performing below the required standard. Bring the focus of the conversation back to this group of people who are the performers, and educate the problem holder on the link between performance and capability. There is plenty of material in this book to help you do that, and you could even use the mechanic story to make the point. You need to develop a common understanding as to precisely how you are using the word capability.

Then it's a simple step to say that if these people are not doing what is required of them, why not? What are the barriers that are stopping them doing the desired behaviours rather than their current poor performance behaviours?

Introduce the idea of using the Ishikawa cause-effect diagram as a tool to analyse the system and discover the root causes of the lack of capability which is leading to the poor performance. Many people have heard of this well-known business tool, for which the more common name is the fishbone diagram. However, in my experience, even if they have heard of it, few have ever actually used it.

There are a number of other tools or processes that you could use at this point to analyse what is happening and find the barriers to capability. I recommend using the fishbone diagram simply because it is quite well known, and is seen as a serious and well-tested business tool, rather than something that is solely used by L&D. Remember, L&D needs to meet other people in the business in their world and on their terms, so using their tools to diagnose the root cause of their problems makes good sense. Using the fishbone diagram in collaboration with people outside L&D will give them the added comfort of feeling that you know what you are doing, which will help them buy into the output you get from using the tool.

The cause-effect diagram was popularised by Kaoru Ishikawa, who was a quality manager in the Kawasaki shipyards in the 1960s. Although originally used for investigating quality issues, it also works well for investigating many other problems, including those involving capability. The cause-effect diagram offers a way to uncover, in successive layers of detail, the root causes that contribute to a particular effect.

The fishbone diagrams are so-called because of their distinctive shape. To create a diagram, draw a line with the obvious problem written in a box at one end. Then draw lines at 45 degrees to the 'backbone', for ribs, and label them with types of cause. Ribs can have any suitable label, but these often have something to do with people, money, machines, materials, environment, measurements, processes and product. You can have as many ribs as you like, but keeping it simple avoids overlap and confusion. Then add any sub-causes you can think of to each rib. One way to do this is to keep asking 'Why?' and when you have an answer, ask 'Why?' again.

In our case, the effect we are investigating is a worker's lack of capability to do a specific task at the point of work. We want to know the things that are causing this lack of capability.

In Chapter 4 we looked at the different components of capability. The four components that are internal to the worker are knowledge, skills, mindset and physiology, and to this is added the fifth component, which is the environment within which the worker is performing.

Use the cause-effect diagram twice: once for the first four components, and then for the environment. There are several reasons why I suggest doing it this way.

1. It explicitly separates the causes of lack of capability into two primary groups, those that relate directly to the workers, and everything else, which relates to the environment. It is almost certain the problem holder has not considered this sort of split before.
2. Using a simple fishbone with four predetermined ribs allows you to 'train' the problem holder on how to use the fishbone diagram. The second diagram, relating to the environment, can be much more complex.
3. Their initial solution, which was probably a request for training, is focused on 'fixing' the workers. By creating a fishbone diagram that is focused on the workers, you are matching their current thinking, and they think you are looking in the right place.

Ideally, use a large whiteboard – one that is big enough to hold both fishbone diagrams at once. There are a lot of advantages to being able to see both diagrams at once; essentially, it enables you to look for common themes and to see where most of the root causes are clustered. In addition, when you can both stand in front of whiteboard, there is a sense of co-creation and collaboration. If a large whiteboard is not available, you can make do with flipchart paper on a table. However you create the fishbone diagrams, make sure you have a way of saving them for future reference.

Set up the first fishbone diagram with the four internal aspects of capability. As you draw the four ribs and label them with knowledge, skills, mindset and physiology, you need to talk about these words to ensure that you have a common understanding of what they mean in this context. It is useful to have a story to explain what each of these words mean. You can use my stories from Chapter 4, or you can use your own stories. The latter would probably be better. I use the road signs story because that resonates with me; I remember the flashing blue lights, and I can tell that story with sincerity and from personal experience.

You can tackle the addition of information to the fishbone diagram in a couple of ways. One is to look at the title of the rib, for example knowledge, and ask the question, 'What knowledge is missing that is stopping them doing what we want them to do?' The other way is to ask a general question on what is stopping them doing what we want them to do and then decide which rib it belongs on, or if it belongs on the second, environmental fishbone diagram.

If they are still uncertain as to how a fishbone diagram functions, take one rib (for example, knowledge) and say,

> 'Mr Manager, you have a bunch of people who are not doing what you want them to do. We have figured out what you do want them to do instead, so the question now is, is there any knowledge they must have and that must be available on instant recall that they currently don't have, but need in order to do what you want them to do?'

When they mention a specific piece of knowledge (for example, product specifications), make sure it really is needed on recall rather than available from easy-to-access resources. The expert often thinks that people need a huge amount of knowledge, just because that's what they can recall, when actually much of that could just as easily be outsourced to an external resource, which could be a database, the intranet, or a post-it note stuck on the wall.

If they come up with a piece of knowledge that genuinely is required, think about whether it is just one or a few individuals who are missing this knowledge, or everyone. And now ask why that knowledge is missing. What is the cause of it being absent? And whatever the answer is, ask 'why?' again, to drill down into the sequence of causes. Sometimes this simple question is not sufficient and you may need to be a bit more specific, asking a question such as 'why is this process failing at this point?'

Before you have the meeting, it is worth sitting down with a colleague and using the fishbone tool to practise with the same problem. If you can second-guess what will come up in the pending meeting, you will be able to guide and facilitate the process more effectively. But no matter how much you prepare, always remember that the problem holder is the expert in their area and they will be able to add things to the fishbone diagram that you cannot think of.

At some point, people will keep drifting into environmental factors when they are working on the first fishbone diagram. It is now time to start the second one, for the environment, at which point you can work on both diagrams concurrently. Because of the huge variability in environmental factors, you will need to create your own 'bare bones' diagram for the environment, and label the main ribs to suit the problem you are investigating. It is a good idea if you have prepared two or three ribs that you can put up as a starter. Some obvious common environmental factors are process, IT, people resources, and physical resources. Then you need to work with them to figure out what the other possible root causes could be. What are the other areas where there are barriers that stop workers from doing what you want them to do, or what is present that is forcing them to do things that you don't want them to do.

This is where some preparation can be helpful so that when you come to the meeting you already have an idea of what at least some of the main ribs on the environmental fishbone diagram will be. You will also find that, as you work on some ribs, you will end up realising you missed something on one you worked on earlier. In effect, therefore, there is no set sequence to go through; instead, you should be prepared to go with the flow and the conversation. There is an iterative aspect to running these diagrams.

Make sure the problem holder understands that this is only a model and therefore not true and that the two of you are artificially separating components of capability. There will therefore be grey areas where the root cause on one rib might well loop onto another, or you could put the root cause onto two ribs. This is okay because it is all about getting clarity, rather than having an exact and perfect fishbone diagram.

A fishbone diagram is never really finished, because there is always more detail that can be added. Part of the skill of using the tool is knowing when to stop, which is when you have enough detail for your purposes. At this stage, do not go too deep. It is better to move on to other ribs on the fish rather than dwell too much on one.

When you have drilled down far enough, so that a solution for the cause-effect chain is becoming apparent, stop and move onto the next rib. Do not get into a discussion at this point about the solution. Keep looking for more causes, because there will almost always be more than one, and usually many. Performance problems are seldom simple, which is one of the reasons they become problems in the first place.

By now the problem holder should be comfortable working with the fishbone diagram, and in my experience they are also by now eager to use it, because it is already giving them fresh insights into a problem that they have been struggling with. Remember that they are the expert for their area of work, so as far as possible you should facilitate more than input. This helps them understand that they are still the problem holder. It is their problem, not yours. What they started out doing was wanting you to take the problem away from them by taking people away to a training room. So keep subtly reminding them that they are responsible for their problem.

As the fishbone diagrams develop, the problem holder is likely to be somewhat surprised at the various different root causes that start to emerge from the exercise. The visibility of these different root causes will start loosening their hold on their original solution, which was probably training. In my experience, the higher proportion of significant causes of most problems will come from the second, environmental, fish. This is likely to be something of a revelation to the problem holder, who has so far been blaming his people and their lack of competence for the problem.

Just take a moment and consider your own recent experiences when you have been unable to do a task. How much of your inability to do the task was the result of you not having sufficient knowledge or skills, and how much was due to environmental factors. For most people, most of the time, the reason they cannot do a task is because something in their environment stops them from doing it.

As you build the fishbone diagrams, in many cases there won't be enough in terms of cause on the knowledge and skills ribs to explain the lack of capability and performance. It is at this point that the problem holder, at least in their own mind, will start to realise that their position in asking for training is untenable. Unless it is evident from the fishbone diagram that significant elements of knowledge and skills are missing, and that the appropriate way to create those skills and that knowledge is a training course, then it will be dawning on the problem holder that training is not the solution. They may or may not voice this thought.

By the time you are progressing through the second fishbone diagram, I guarantee they will be saying things like 'There is a lot more going on here than I thought.' In effect, they will be realising that the situation is far more complex than they originally thought and in some respects very different.

Solutions

Your output from the two fishbone diagrams is a list of probable root causes. These are the barriers that are getting in the way of people being capable at the point of work, and are therefore the barriers to acceptable performance. I like to use the word barrier rather than root cause, because a barrier seems like something that is getting in the way and that could be changed or moved, whereas a root cause has a sense of permanence about it.

By the way, it is most unlikely that you now have a complete list of barriers. You need to signal this to the problem holder by saying something like 'I bet if we asked some of the other people involved with this, they would have more to add.'

Write down the list of barriers you have so far, and do some initial prioritisation. Mark the ones that probably have more impact, either because they are significant in their own right or because they cause other barriers.

Now brainstorm a few possible solutions for eliminating these barriers. It is absolutely essential that at this point you do not agree to provide any of these solutions. Do not shoot from the hip, no matter how urgent the need seems to be.

Some of the solutions you come up with together will be very quick and easy to implement, and possibly even free, in which case the problem holder may well just go and implement them, which is absolutely fine. These could be small changes in process and procedure, for example, or introducing a very simple job aid.

As with any brainstorming process, you need to bring in a dose of creativity, so dust off your creativity techniques. For example, use a reversal technique and ask the question, 'How could we make it much worse?' and then flip your answer. This will often give you insights into a deeper root cause, or a future problem that is lurking in the wings.

Now is the time to put a challenge in front of the problem holder. Challenge them to come up with three different ways to tackle a root cause or barrier to performance. This is very much about having empathy with the performer. If I am the performer, what would help me perform better? What would I need to perform up to the required standard? Given that I need something, what are three different ways that I could receive or be given this extra something? How would I want to receive it? What method would be most cost effective? What method would be most efficient? How can I interact with other performers to get it? How did the good performers, if there are any, get good at what they do? Is there a better, more efficient way, to get good at the task? Is there some way to change the task to make it easier? Why are we doing the task? What does it feel like to do the task?

This is particularly important when you are looking at the knowledge or skills barrier. The temptation will be to just think of training as the solution, but in a large proportion of cases a classroom intervention will not be the best way to tackle that lack of knowledge or lack of skill. Structured and facilitated on-the-job learning could easily be a better solution than putting people in a classroom, although there will of course still be some times when a classroom solution is absolutely the best answer.

When you are considering learning as a solution to a knowledge or skills barrier, it can be useful put this in the context of the five moments of learning need, an idea developed by Con Gottfredson and Bob Mosher.[57]

1. When people are learning how to do something for the first time (New).
2. When people are expanding the breadth and depth of what they have learned (More).

3. When they need to act on what they have learned, which includes planning what they will do, remembering what they may have forgotten, or adapting the performance to a unique situation (Apply).
4. When problems arise, or things break or don't work the way they were intended (Solve).
5. When people need to learn a new way of doing something that requires them to change skills that are deeply ingrained in their performance practices (Change).

Understanding which moment of need the learning must address will help determine what sort of learning solution would be appropriate.

It is important to add a little bit of time into the process at this point to avoid the temptation to jump to a premature conclusion on the ideal set of solutions. Now is the time to reflect on what has happened and what has come out of the meeting and doing the analysis. Be aware, however, that the performance consultancy process is not yet finished.

During the course of this meeting you need to keep a close watch on time because you do not want to exceed the hour that you have agreed. Make sure that you get to the point where you have a brainstormed list of possible solutions, and that is your endpoint to this meeting.

Finish the meeting by thanking the person or people for their input and creativity; stress that their input and expertise was extremely valuable in getting to the core of what was going on. You need to set some expectations on what will happen next and what will be expected of them. Encourage people to reflect and sleep on what has transpired.

1. Ask them to reflect on what has been discovered during the meeting and to let you know if they come up with any further ideas. If the problem holder has had a number of surprises during the meeting, they will almost certainly reflect on those.
2. Explain to them that you will need to visit and speak with the workers and their managers, who are at the heart of the performance problem.
3. Let the problem holder know that another meeting will be required soon in order to get together with other stakeholders who will be affected, and agree a plan of action.

It is very tempting at this point to confirm what you will do as a solution, because it looks tantalisingly close and because you have this list of root causes written out. Do not be deceived. This list is almost certainly incomplete and the only way you can complete it is to talk with other people who are on the stakeholder diagram. So far you have only one person's view of what is going on, and they may well have been hiding or carefully not mentioning some aspects of the situation to protect themselves. Remember, the problem holder is often one of the causes of the problem, or a barrier to performance. This is unlikely to have surfaced during this meeting, and won't be visible until you speak with other stakeholders.

The reputation and brand of L&D is at stake here. If you 'solutioneer' at this point, before you have fully investigated the performance problem, you are falling into the same trap that ensnared the problem holder.

Notice that we have never at any point challenged them on their training solution, we have simply made things visible to them in a way that lets them confirm or reject it. We have done everything under the guise of working with them to make their solution better.

Remember, the outcome of the meeting is to align their wants with their real needs. We do that by exposing to them what they actually need so they can see it for themselves. Their real need will now become what they want and they will abandon their original want, whatever that was, because they will realise it is not what they actually need.

Chapter 8

Stage 3 – After the meeting

*Most people define learning too narrowly as mere 'problem-solving',
so they focus on identifying and correcting errors in the external
environment. Solving problems is important. But if learning is to
persist, managers and employees must also look inward. They need
to reflect critically on their own behaviour, identify the ways they
often inadvertently contribute to the organisation's problems, and
then change how they act.*

Chris Argyris

The primary outcomes of this third stage are to complete the diagnostics,
agree the solutions is to be used, and start taking action. In effect, the
performance consultancy process will morph into a project management
process.

If all has gone well during the first two stages, you will by now have a good
foundation in place. The problem holder will have realised that their initial
requested solution would not have solved their problem, although of course
it could end up being a part of the eventual solution. They will no longer be

interacting with you as an order taker. They will see you as an ally and someone who can help them deal with their performance problem. You also now have a huge amount of information about the situation, about the probable barriers that are getting in the way of people performing effectively, and some initial ideas on how to deal with those barriers.

You need to think carefully about how to take the process forward. This will depend on the scale of the future programme to implement a solution in terms of the costs of failure and the benefits of success. It depends on the number of people who are involved. You may also need to deal with the problem holder's boss, who may still be jumping up and down wanting a training course.

So far most of the information that you have has come from the problem holder, who is the manager who is responsible for the performance of that particular part of the organisation. That is only one side of the story. It would not be wise to move forward at this stage into choosing and implementing one or more solutions without getting other sides to the story. There will be several groups of stakeholders with whom you should speak to get a balanced view of the problem and its effects, and gather further information that could prove relevant and useful:

1. The workers who are at the heart of the problem; that is, the people who are the performers who, for one reason or another, are not capable of performing at an adequate level
2. The managers of the performers
3. The manager of the problem holder
4. People in other operational areas who are affected by the current problem
5. People in other operational areas who will be affected by solving the problem
6. People who will probably need to be involved with the solutions.

The performers

I am continually surprised by how many times I see solutions to a performance problem put in place without any dialogue with the performers. Perhaps it is because management thinks it totally understands what is happening at the point of work. This is never the case. The performers have a unique view of how they do things, what makes their job easy or difficult, who they rely on, and what they need in order to be able to do their job more easily.

Other than the fact that they have a huge amount of useful information that they can feed into the process of deciding on the actions needed to solve the problem, they are the people who will be taking many of those actions. The performers buy-in to the chosen solutions will usually be crucial to the success of those solutions, and including them in the process will go a long way to achieving that buy-in.

Be careful in your approach to the organisational unit or team that has been defined as underperforming. All you have so far is what you have been told by the problem holder, and although I would hope it is accurate from their point of view, it may well be very different to the story you will get from the performers. The problem holder themselves may well be a significant contributor to the poor performance, and of course this is unlikely to have surfaced during your meeting with them. An open mind and a willingness to hear all sides of the story is essential. You need the balance of views between the problem holder and the people who are perceived as the problem.

You should, of course, ask the problem holder for permission to approach members of his team. This is a reasonable request and can hardly be refused; however, he may attach some conditions to your interaction with them if the amount of time you are requesting with them would interrupt their productivity. By the response you get, you will learn a lot about the relationship between the problem holder and their team. Sometimes, their response may also indicate that the problem holder could be hiding information that they fear will come to the surface when you discuss the performance issue with the team.

If the group of people who are underperforming covers a whole organisational unit, there may well be one or more layers of management between the problem holder and the performers. Ask the problem holder who would be the best people to speak with, and also ask why he recommends those particular individuals as a good source of information. It can be helpful if the problem holder sends an email or message asking for cooperation from the team members when you approach them.

Your first step is to have a brief informal discussion with the recommended team members, plus a couple of others who were not recommended, in order to get a sense of whether they describe the problem in the same way as the problem holder, or whether their view is significantly different. Now that you have some idea of what extra information they can offer, you can decide how much time you need to spend getting their input. You can also decide how to go about getting information, whether it should be through informal chats, for example, or a structured interview process, or questionnaires or facilitated group sessions.

However you decide to proceed, be aware that they may be reluctant to reveal the kind of information that is needed in order to make an accurate diagnosis. It is possible that systematic distortions will occur within the information they give. The direction of these distortions will depend on the climate of the organisation. If the climate is one of distrust and insecurity, respondents will most likely hide any damaging information from you because of fear of blame. This is something we have seen repeatedly in the misadventures of whistle blowers. All the team members may view the interview, survey or test as an invasion of their privacy and provide minimal answers or distortions based on what they consider to be the expected or safe responses. If the climate is one of high trust, respondents are likely to view contact with you as an opportunity to get all their gripes off their chests, leading to an exaggeration of whatever problems may exist.

It should also be borne in mind that in any human system, the process of diagnosis is itself an intervention of unknown consequence. Your interaction with the team will probably generate some behavioural changes within the team in relation to the problem area.

In order to talk with the performers effectively, you need the background of the preceding process. If you just go to them first, without the background, you will get value from the discussion, but nothing like as much if you go prepared, having done the performance consultancy process as described. The fact that you have obviously researched the issues is another plus, because they will realise that you do care, and that you do already know quite a lot about what is going on. They will also feel that they are contributing to a genuine investigation rather than being asked simply because it is politically correct to do so.

Informal chats

When you have an informal and off the record chat with one of the performers, there are a few questions you can use as prompts to help you structure that conversation:

- What awareness of the performance problem do they have?
- What is their view of the performance problem? What emotion does this bring up within them: frustration, anger, resignation, surprise or indifference, or something else?
- What do they think should be happening instead of what is happening?
- Is their view of what 'good' looks like the same as the problem holder's view? If not, why not? (Explain your understanding of what good looks like, and discuss the difference.)
- Does the problem holder's view of what good looks like make sense to them? Or do they consider it silly or impossible?
- What needs to happen/change in order for the desired way of doing things to be possible?
- What currently frustrates them?
- What they tolerating now that used to frustrate them?
- What barriers are there that get in the way of them doing their jobs to the required standard? (Discuss the list of barriers that you came up with in the meeting with the problem holder.)
- Who else is involved with this, outside the direct team?
- Are there others involved who are in other silos in the business?
- Can they add to the stakeholder diagram?
- Can things be simplified without adding undue risk? For example, can the process be simplified?

In addition, you can...

- Find out what changes have been tried before, and ask why they didn't work
- Mention a few of the proposed solutions that came from the meeting with the problem holder, and ask if those solutions seem reasonable
- Ask about the management they experience from their team leader, and their line managers.

This is quite a list to go through, but it is well worthwhile. Something that is sure to happen is that many other issues that seem unrelated to the current performance problem will get mentioned. Remember that you are working with a system here, and anything that affects the team and its members will affect their productivity.

Group sessions

It is also possible to talk to the performers as a group and facilitate a discussion around the points mentioned above. An advantage of this is the potential for the free flow of ideas; it also gives a high level of visibility to the diagnostics process, which makes even those who were not involved with the discussions feel that their voice is being heard, because their colleagues were part of the process.

In a group session, you can use the fishbone diagram as a way to get active involvement from the performers. They will have a sense of ownership of the decision as to what actually are the root causes. Following on from that, they will gain a sense of ownership of the solution that is put in place to tackle the root causes.

Another advantage of using the fishbone diagram on a whiteboard is that you are pushing the problem out to one side and then looking at it from a distance. This is a very useful technique when the problem, or the solution to the problem, is seen as a significant threat to the people you're talking with. Take the problem; pin it on the wall, then stand back and look at it together. It is much less threatening to talk about 'that problem over there' than to face someone and say 'you have a problem'.

There is, however, a disadvantage to running a facilitated group session and this is the danger of groupthink or of the session being hijacked and pulled off course by one or two vocal people. Another disadvantage is that the group may come up with a solution that they insist is the absolute, only and best solution, which can give rise to ill feeling if some other solution is then chosen instead of theirs.

The managers

One of the root causes that is on almost every performance consultancy fishbone diagram I have ever seen is poor management. Managers are responsible for so many of the components of capability that the quality of management should always be under scrutiny when there is a performance problem.

This must be taken into consideration when discussing the performance problem with them. Many managers will point the finger everywhere else except at themselves. Others will wallow in self-blame. Still others will be oblivious to the role they should have been playing in the performance of their team and may actually be quite surprised and affronted if someone starts suggesting that they could have done better.

When discussing the performance problem with a manager, you can use the same list of bullet points mentioned above. Just be aware of the dynamic that is introduced because at least some responsibility for the poor performance must rest with them. Having said that, there is every chance that the people who manage them, and so on up the hierarchy, are also failing in their ability to provide an adequate management service to the people they manage.

As with the performers, you could gather a few of the team leaders or line managers together and facilitate them through using the fishbone diagram to help them produce a list of root causes or barriers to performance. Then go through the list of barriers and ask them what could be done about these. It is the same solutions brainstorming approach that you would have used with the original problem holder.

As you enter the list of possible solutions, ask who would be best placed to implement each solution. Inevitably, they will realise that many of the solutions are within their remit, and with that they will also recognise their own part in creating the performance problem, or allowing it to exist. What happens next will depend on the quality of people who have those management roles. Will they go into denial, or will they commit to learning a better way and step up to their role as a manager?

When you are going through this kind of process with a group of managers, it is better if all the people in the group are at the same hierarchical level. If their boss or another senior manager is in the room, they are unlikely to be as open or honest. It is also possible that the senior manager will start directing them to do certain things or behave a certain way, based on what has come out of the fishbone diagram and the list of solutions. It is much better if the group of managers collectively decide how they will respond to the new information, and then present this to their line managers as something they would like to do. In effect, they are taking ownership, and this is something you should encourage.

When you are looking at the various solutions, notice which ones are quickly dismissed by the managers. Is it really because that solution is a bad one, or is it because implementing that solution will result in some kind of loss for the managers?

It is possible to look at the quality of management as a performance problem, and run that through the performance consultancy as an issue in its own right. If it becomes apparent that poor management is one of the key factors for a team or organisational unit failing, then the next step may will be to look at management as the primary performance problem rather than, for example, the number of widgets being produced by the team.

The manager of the problem holder

It is unlikely that the problem holder is the CEO, so there will be someone who is the boss of the problem holder, and of course that may even be the CEO. They are definitely a stakeholder, and their opinion matters, not least because there is every chance that they are the person who will need to sign off the budget on any solution that is decided.

You need to find out how important this particular performance problem is to the senior manager. Is it something on the edge of their awareness, or is it something that keeps them awake at night? Do they want to be directly involved with any solution in a hands-on way, or do they just want to know what has been done and what the results are? You would not ask this directly, but do they trust the problem holder to handle the problem? How is this problem likely to impact the larger strategic goals that this senior manager is responsible for?

Your discussion with the senior manager will have a big impact on how they view the value of L&D and your input into their department, so be prepared for this discussion and think carefully about the points you want to cover in the time that you have been given. You will probably find it necessary to give them a précis of the results that came out of the meeting you had with the problem holder, and subsequent conversations you had with the performers. It is important that they understand that there are a number of possible barriers or root causes to the performance issue because they may well have the 'training is the answer' mindset. You need to get them to the point where they understand that there is likely to be a range of solutions, addressing a range of barriers to performance.

Do not be drawn into making promises, or confirming what solutions will be put in place. Just say that you are still going through a performance diagnosis process and you are still gathering information before making recommendations.

Talk about the next steps you intend to take, and ask for their support. Also ask what level of reporting they want and how closely they want to be involved with any further meetings or decisions.

People in other silos

Almost every performance problem in an organisation will have a knock-on effect on other departments that are downstream in the process flow. This may be significant to them in terms of their own productivity, or be little more than an annoyance. In some cases, they will not even be aware that it is affecting what they do because the long-standing nature of the performance problem means that no one knows any different.

Ask the other stakeholders what the performance problem is costing them, because this may add to the overall cost of the problem across the organisation. A larger overall cost will make a difference to the urgency of fixing the problem, and also affect what budget could or should be allocated to fixing the problem.

Also ask if they have a similar problem in their own department. It may well be that some of the solutions that you develop for the original problem holder could be useful to other departments, and there may be an economy of scale available, and other budgets you can call on. For example, one of the barriers may well be a cultural issue that is endemic across the whole organisation, and has a negative effect on the productivity of all the departments. A solution that addresses this cultural issue would probably be useful to all departments.

Another question to ask is how these other departments would be affected when the original performance problem is solved. For example, if the performance problem was too many rejects from a manufacturing line, you need to consider whether, when the number of rejects is dramatically reduced, downstream processes, such as the assembly line or the paint shop, will be able to handle the higher volume.

Solutions costs

By now you will have a list of barriers, and an even longer list of solutions that could be put in place to remove those barriers. Clearly, when the decision is made on which solutions to use, one of the deciding factors will be the cost of each solution. You therefore need to get at least some information about the cost of each of the possible solutions. Some of these costs you will be able to come up with on your own, but many others will involve input from other departments or even external suppliers, so you will need to have discussions with people who could be involved in delivering solutions.

At this stage, you are not looking for definitive quotes or detailed proposals from anybody. You just need some ballpark figures that you can take into the next meeting.

The next meeting

By now you will have gathered a huge amount of information about the performance problem.

- You will have a good understanding of the problem from the perspective of most of the stakeholders.
- You will have a reasonable indication of the costs to the business of the problem.
- You will have a list or diagram of the stakeholders, both internal and external.
- You will have an understanding of what a successful outcome would look like to the different stakeholders.
- You will have a prioritised list of the root causes that are generating the poor performance.
- You will have a list of the barriers that are stopping workers from being capable at the point of work.
- You will have a list of potential solutions to deal with those barriers.

- You will have some rough costings for each of the solutions on the list.

The next step is to convene a meeting with a sufficient number of the stakeholders to allow decisions to be made on which solutions to put in place and how to proceed. The agenda for the meeting would be a presentation from you, the performance consultant, on the bullet points above. You could also write a report on the information and circulate it prior to the meeting.

The outcome of the meeting is to decide on the list of actions, and who will undertake those actions. In effect, the performance consultancy process draws to a close and transforms into a project management process.

You have probably talked with everyone in the meeting about this problem, and about your findings, so much of what you would present to them would not be news. The reason for the presentation is to refresh their memories, and also to ensure that everyone in the room is now working from the same data – the information that has come out of the performance consultancy process.

The discussion will centre on the list of solutions. I would recommend that this is a free-flowing discussion about the solutions, how to prioritise them, whether the costs seem reasonable, which ones should be grouped together, which ones can be tested easily, which ones can be implemented immediately and so on. Use the wisdom of the group, and all the different perspectives in the room, to start homing in on which solutions to use and in which order to introduce them.

You should also be looking at the consequences of the preferred solutions. The best way to do this is to take each one in turn and ask these four questions:

1. What will happen if we implement this solution?
2. What won't happen if we implement this solution?
3. What will happen if we don't implement this solution?
4. What won't happen if we don't implement this solution?

Many solutions will have unintended and sometimes unpredictable side effects. It is also important to consider how different solutions will impact each other when implemented either sequentially or in parallel.

If you have a large list of causes, it's almost certain you will also have a large shopping list of potential solutions. It should also be borne in mind that dealing with some of the major root causes will automatically remove some of the smaller peripheral ones. The problem must be looked at as a system composed of a number of components, so you must consider how inputs to the system affect each other, and affect the outputs of the system.

If enough time has passed since your first meeting with the problem holder, some of the stakeholders may have already taken some action, implementing some of the quick and cheap solutions that were identified. If so, ask them to report to the meeting on how their intervention affected the problem. This will give you some insight into how the system responds to intervention, and how you can measure or describe the responses of the system to intervention. Inevitably solutions sometimes create further problems. According to Chris Argyris, some 60 per cent of our problems are the result of previous solutions.

Depending on the size of the problem and the number of potential solutions to be implemented, you may be discussing the possibility that quite a large programme will be needed to pull everything together. That obviously raises the question as to who will be the programme manager, so the meeting should agree on who will handle that role and who will be the executive sponsor.

If the change involves a small number of stakeholders, and the budget is not significantly large, then the current problem holder may well be the best person to be the project manager. In this case, they clearly retain ownership of the problem and responsibility for solving it. If the change involves a large number of stakeholders across different parts of the organisation, and there is a significant amount of money at stake, then someone who has experience of managing programmes that are in effect a portfolio of smaller projects should be put in charge. If the solutions that have been agreed are mostly to be delivered by L&D then it may be appropriate for someone from L&D to be the project manager. If this is agreed, then be sure that the problem holder is seen as the sponsor for the project.

As with any programme that is going to cost the organisation money and time, it is essential that there is some way to measure success. During the consultancy process, you have discussed with people what a successful resolution of the performance problem will look like to them in terms of observable behaviours and quantitative measures. You now have the raw material for designing some success criteria, but it's important that these are pulled together into an agreed format.

In effect, you are building a change programme and it is change skills that now need to be brought into play. The performance consultancy process is finished, at least for this particular problem.

Chapter 9

The role of the manager

The supposition is prevalent the world over that there would be no problems in production or service if only our production workers would do their jobs in the way that they were taught. Pleasant dreams. The workers are handicapped by the system, and the system belongs to the management.

W. Edwards Deming

Studies continue to show that an employee's direct supervisor has the greatest impact on their performance and motivation, and loyalty to the organisation. You can't talk about performance in the workplace without talking about managers, for two simple reasons:

1. The managers are almost certain to be one of the root causes for the poor performance on the fishbone diagram
2. The managers are almost certain to be key players in the implementation of any solution to tackle the poor performance.

I often talk about managers having superpowers. Whenever somebody becomes a manager, they automatically get their superpowers. They don't need to undergo some kind of traumatic event like being hit by a strange meteorite, or bitten by a mutant spider. They just need to be promoted to manage some other people, and they then have their superpowers as long as they remain a manager.

If you are thinking that the idea of superpowers for managers is some idle fantasy, think again. Here is some 'proof' from research done at Stanford University. In their paper 'The Value of Bosses'[58], Edward Lazear, Kathryn Shaw and Christopher Stanton came up with the following conclusions...

"By using data from a large service-oriented company, it is possible to examine the effects of bosses on their workers' productivity and to compare them to individual and peer effects. The primary findings are:

1. Bosses are important and vary in productivity. Replacing a boss who is in the lower 10% of boss quality with one who is in the upper 10% of boss quality increases a team's total output by about the same amount as would adding one worker to a nine-member team.
2. The marginal product of a boss is about twice as large as the marginal product of a typical worker. The ratio is consistent with difference in compensation levels.
3. Bosses are the only 'peer' that matters. Peer effects are small or zero, whereas boss effects are substantial.
4. Good bosses increase the productivity of many different types of workers. Bosses who are good for older workers are also good for new workers.
5. The difference between the effect of good and bad bosses on high-quality workers is greater than that on lower quality workers, which suggests that to the extent that the same boss is good for both, the assignment of the good boss should be made to the higher quality workers."

Their research shows that the effect of workers is additive, whereas the effect of bosses is multiplicative. And of course this multiplicative effect can be either positive or negative.

The UK Investors in People organisation carried out their IIP Leadership Horizon Survey 2014 and offered the following results:

- One in eight workers – equivalent to 3.7 million workers in the UK – could not name one quality they liked about their boss
- Of those who said they didn't have a good relationship with their manager, 43 per cent said they considered looking for a new job as a result
- 36 per cent feel less motivated to do a good job for the company.

A report by the Corporate Leadership Council, *Improving Talent Management Outcomes*[59], had this to say about the effect of managers...

"Many managers unknowingly undermine employee performance. Line managers directly influence a majority of the key drivers of employee performance, improving or destroying performance by up to 40%."

Peter Drucker said "So much of what we call management consists in making it difficult for people to work."

What is fascinating about the vast majority of managers is that they are completely unaware that they have these superpowers. This is despite the fact that these superpowers are active whether they intend to use them or not. They cannot be switched off.

Now, of course, you are wondering what these superpowers are, especially if you are a manager. It is simple really, if you think about it. Every manager has an incredibly powerful ability to manage the environment that surrounds the people in their team. In the previous chapters, we have seen how important environmental factors are to the capability of people at their point of work. Now think about the other factors of capability, which are knowledge, skills, mindset and physiology. Other than the last one, a manager has a huge impact on these by the way they interact with the people on their team.

The way the manager behaves will always affect the capability of the people on their team and that effect can be positive or negative. That is, their superpowers can just as easily render someone incapable, rather than capable. This is actually very dangerous when you consider that they do not realise that they have these powers, or if they do, just how powerful these powers really are. A manager can inadvertently do a huge amount of damage in terms of the capability, and therefore performance, of their team, without understanding that it is actually them that is causing the problem. All too often, they do not know what they do not know. They operate with a very limited view of what management is all about, and are oblivious to their real role, and their real power. They are truly unconsciously incompetent.

If you have been keeping up with the activities of the superheroes in the comics and films, you will realise that it is considered immoral for any person who has been endowed with superpowers not to use those powers for the greater good. You will also realise that in most cases the superheroes have some kind of mentor who helps them come to terms with their power, and the moral obligations that it brings.

If we think of it this way, then we have two things to do:

1. Help managers become aware of the awesome power they have to manage capability
2. Help them use their power to become effective capability managers.

Actually there is a third thing we also need to do, and that is to help them decide whether they are capable of wielding their superpowers effectively, or whether they should hang up their cape and leave the superhero stuff to someone else. Not everyone has what it takes; in fact, surveys and research by Gallup suggest that only one in ten people can make the most of their superpowers. Randall Beck and James Harter reported on the Gallup results on the Harvard Business Review blog.[60] They say...

> "If great managers seem scarce, it's because the talent required to be one is rare. Gallup finds that great managers have the following talents:
>
> - They **motivate** every single employee to take action and engage them with a compelling mission and vision.
> - They have the **assertiveness** to drive outcomes and the ability to overcome adversity and resistance.
> - They create a culture of clear **accountability.**
> - They build **relationships** that create trust, open dialogue, and full transparency.
> - They **make decisions** that are based on productivity, not politics.
>
> "Gallup's research reveals that about one in ten people possess all these necessary traits. While many people are endowed with some of them, few

have the unique combination of talents needed to help a team achieve excellence in a way that significantly improves a company's performance. These 10 per cent, when put in manager roles, naturally engage team members and customers, retain top performers, and sustain a culture of high productivity. Combined, they contribute about 48 per cent higher profit to their companies than average managers.

"It's important to note that another two in ten exhibit some characteristics of basic managerial talent and can function at a high level if their company invests in coaching and developmental plans for them."

Clearly the recruitment or promotion programmes that focus on technical skills or company tenure will not find, other than by chance, people with the above five talents. Beck and Carter go on to say...

"It's important to note – especially in the current economic climate – that finding great managers doesn't depend on market conditions or the current labour force. Large companies have approximately one manager for every ten employees, and Gallup finds that one in ten people possess the inherent talent to manage. When you do the math, it's likely that someone on each team has the talent to lead. But given our findings, chances are that it's not the manager. More likely, it's an employee with high managerial potential waiting to be discovered.

"The good news is that sufficient management talent exists in every company – it's often hiding in plain sight. Leaders should maximise this potential by choosing the right person for the next management role using predictive analytics to guide their identification of talent."

So perhaps we should be saying there are four things we need to do:

1. Help managers become aware of the awesome power they have to manage capability
2. Help them use their power to become effective capability managers
3. Help them decide whether they are capable of wielding their superpowers effectively, or whether they should hang up their cape and leave the superhero stuff to someone else
4. Find people within the workforce who have the talents to wield managerial superpowers effectively.

In addition to the investigative role of the performance consultant when they use the process we have outlined in the previous chapters, there is also a coaching or mentoring role in terms of helping managers with their superpowers. The performance consultant should help the manager find their own superhero style so they can fight for truth, justice and superior performance.

A classic article in the Harvard Business Review explores the irrefutable connection between quality of management and quality of employee performance. In 'The Set-Up-To-Fail Syndrome', authors Jean-François Manzoni and Jean-Louis Barsoux[61] say...

> "When an employee fails – or even just performs poorly – managers typically do not blame themselves. The employee doesn't understand the work, a manager might contend. Or the employee isn't driven to succeed, can't set priorities, or won't take direction. Whatever the reason, the problem is assumed to be the employee's fault – and the employee's responsibility.

> "But is it? Sometimes, of course, the answer is yes. Some employees are not up to their assigned tasks and never will be, for lack of knowledge, skill, or simple desire. But sometimes – and we would venture to say often – an employee's poor performance can be blamed largely on his boss.

> "Perhaps 'blamed' is too strong a word, but it is directionally correct. In fact, our research strongly suggests that bosses – albeit accidentally and usually with the best intentions – are often complicit in an employee's lack of success."

Performance management

Performance management, in the way it is normally defined, is different to capability management. Performance management brings company strategy to life by making clear the links between individual objectives, team objectives and company objectives. It involves creating a shared vision of the purpose and aims of the organisation; helping each team member understand the part they play in contributing to them, and enhancing the performance of team members by establishing objectives and monitoring progress.

A commonly-used definition of performance management is the set of ongoing management practices that help ensure employees get the direction, feedback and development they need to succeed in their roles.

A successful employee performance management process...

- Aligns goals, ensuring employees clearly know what is expected of them and how their work contributes to the achievement of organisational goals
- Builds competencies, helping cultivate the organisational and job-specific competencies each employee and the organisation need for high performance and success
- Focuses on employee development, helping employees develop and improve so they can be successful, continually improve their performance, increase their knowledge, skills, experience and competence, and progress in their careers
- Engages and empowers employees, inviting each employee to take responsibility for their own performance, development and career progression, while contributing to the organisation's success
- Facilitates a dialog about performance, encouraging a regular, ongoing dialog between employees and managers about expectations, progress, accomplishments, performance and development needs
- Ensures employees get feedback and recognition, providing mechanisms for employees to get the feedback and recognition they need to continually improve and succeed
- Culminates in a formal review (at least once per year), providing an opportunity to gather up, review and document the results of the ongoing dialog about expectations, performance and development
- Improves your bottom line, helping increase productivity, efficiency and skill, lower costs, eliminate duplication of effort and waste, and facilitate the execution of your strategy.

If you look at the books on management and the content of training courses on management, the concept of performance management is typically focused on managing people rather than managing the process or the system within which those people are operating. This focus on people makes it very easy to blame the people for lack of performance, and to think that in some way that people need to be 'fixed' in order for the performance to improve. Performance management becomes managing underperformance.

According to Michael Armstrong in his book *How to Be an Even Better Manager*, now in its eighth edition[62],

> "Performance management is a systematic approach to improving individual and team performance. It embraces the process of performance appraisal but is also concerned with measuring performance. It is based on two simple propositions:
>
> 1. People are most likely to perform well when they know and understand what is expected of them and have taken part in defining these expectations.
> 2. The ability to meet these expectations depends on the level of competence and motivation of individuals and the leadership and support they received from their managers."

Armstrong then goes on to state that performance management takes the form of the continuous normal cycle of management. That is: plan, act, monitor, review and then back to plan. The focus of the remainder of the chapter on performance management in his book is on measurement.

If you look through the chapter headings of Armstrong's book, and indeed any other book that I have seen on management, and I have seen a lot, it is mostly about managing people. Pick up the next few books you find on management and look for yourself at the chapter headings. There is seldom anything that relates directly to managing capability in the way that we have defined it here.

So, there appears to be a rather glaring gap in the way we inform and train the managers in our organisations. And of course that assumes that they are getting any training at all. Research by the CIPD in 2013[63] reveals that 36 per cent of line managers have not received any training for their role. The report goes on to say that efforts to foster positive manager behaviours are being undermined by the lack of a consistent message as to what organisations expect of managers. The research also found that 28 per cent of companies have not taken any action when they have received poor feedback on line managers.

Ksenia Zheltoukhova, a Research Associate at CIPD, said...

"We hear organisations lament the lack and quality of leaders, but we aren't seeing evidence of their commitment to drive good leadership and management practices. For 29 per cent of managers in the CIPD survey 'other priorities' stand in the way of ensuring that the interests of the team members are supported, raising questions about the priorities that managers – and the organisations – attach to the wellbeing of their staff. These findings are a wake-up call for businesses to re-align the systems and structures in place in their organisations to support leadership development.

"Businesses address issues such as poor customer service or faulty machinery straight away, whereas bad management across organisations is tolerated to a shocking degree. In the CIPD survey, 28 per cent of organisations failed to act upon poor feedback on line managers; and nearly half (48 per cent) confessed that individuals were promoted into managerial roles based on their performance record rather than people management or leadership skills. It's time for business to identify and address the roots of bad management, recognising that a more consistent approach to training and supporting leaders at all levels of an organisation is needed to drive sustainable performance."

We can hardly blame the managers. Most of us get to be managers abruptly, without previous experience. Suddenly, we are put in charge of other people's work. We are 'accidental managers'. As a rule, we get promoted because we are particularly good at some *other* job rather than management. From that day on, our personal skills are no longer of prime importance. Our success depends on how well we can get other people to give of their best. We are often left on our own to pick up the new set of skills that we will need to achieve this. The attitude common in many organisations is that managers are born, not made.

Even a small amount of reflection will show the fallacy in this attitude. I have yet to hear of the midwife who holds a new-born child and grandly announces 'it's a manager!'

It is little wonder then that most managers have a rather narrow and possibly even dysfunctional view of performance management and what that means in practice. The piece of the puzzle they are missing is the concept of capability management. When you are managing capability, you are actually managing the underlying causes of the performance you are getting.

Capability management

The Oxford dictionary defines management as 'The process of dealing with or controlling things or people'. Capability management means controlling the capability of the people in your team, or more accurately controlling the factors that affect the capability of the people in your team. This is one of the fundamental steps to take for organisational success. There is a clear line of sight between managing capability and performance. The level of performance underpins the results that are achieved. The results that are achieved are what the stakeholders use to decide whether an organisation is successful in fulfilling its vision, mission and purpose.

The factors that affect capability are critical to organisational success, and this is good news, because we can figure out what they are, and when we know that, we can figure out what to do about them.

Frontline and midline managers are the people who have the most impact on the capability factors, even if they have not yet discovered their superpowers. The best way to mentor them through the discovery and effective use of their power is to use the performance consultancy process with them so they have a growing awareness of their role. Work with them to teach them the components of capability, through the use of the fishbone diagram. Help them understand that by doing this they will begin to see the nuts and bolts of the performance puzzle and how to solve it.

Help them see performance as a system with some components that they can directly manage and control. Too often, managers stand back and measure performance, and when they don't get the numbers they want, they decide their people are incompetent, and focus on knee-jerk solutions to what they perceive as a people problem.

The change I am suggesting requires quite a significant shift in mindset towards a servant-led style of management and leadership. Many managers are happy to have influence (power) over their employees, but far fewer are happy to accept responsibility for their employees, and far fewer still will even consider being accountable to their employees.

Ken Blanchard, co-author of the hugely successful book *The One Minute Manager*[64], is also well-known for his writings about servant leadership – the concept that effective leaders need to serve the needs of their people, instead of looking to be served by them. This idea seems to get lost in the modern workplace, perhaps because there are so few good role models who understand that the basic premise of management is to serve. Just as when you become a parent, there is an awesome responsibility when you become a manager, so it's fortunate indeed that you get some superpowers at the same time.

Every manager should be on a constant quest to find out how best to serve the people on their team to help those people do what they are employed to do. The capability manager needs to keep asking the questions, 'What do you need in order to be able to do your job more effectively?' or 'What barriers are in place that are making it more difficult than necessary to do your job?' or 'What frustrates you at work?' and 'What do you now tolerate that used to frustrate you?'

They should also look for barriers to capability that the performers may not see. They need to stand back to see the larger system and ask 'What is preventing my team or people within my team from being capable of doing the task in front of them when I ask them to do it?' With the speed at which things can affect business, a manager who waits for an employee to announce a problem has waited too long. Each manager needs to become proactive as a capability manager.

Being proactive brings you into the area of preventative management, a concept described by Ferdinand F. Fournies in his book *Why employees don't do what they are supposed to do and what to do about it*[65]. Fournies and his consulting colleagues conducted a study over 25 years in which they gathered information from over 25,000 managers in which they focused on asking the question "Why don't your subordinates do what they are supposed to do?"

They found that most managers could not give a useful or detailed answer to that question, and very often blamed lack of motivation. When they disallowed lack of motivation as an answer, they started to get more detailed responses and realised these answers fell into 16 reasons for non-performance. They said...

> "After working with this list over the years, we noticed something even more interesting: almost all of these reasons for non-performance were controlled by the manager. We also realised that there were two general management causes for most of these reasons for non-performance:

1. The manager did something wrong to or for the employees, or
2. The manager failed to do something right to or for the employees.

"In other words, employee non-performance occurred because of poor management. What followed was the startling realisation that if managers took appropriate action to make the 16 reasons for non-performance go away or prevent them from occurring in the first place, the result would be perfect performance."

This obviously begs the question as to why managers are not addressing the 16 reasons. What they found is that managers were unaware of these distinctions because they thought of performance problems in general terms and described them with metaphors, such as 'not cutting the mustard'. What little analysis they did tended to produce answers such as 'They are not motivated' or 'They are unqualified for the job' or 'They are not the right person for the job'. According to Fournies, many managers operate on the basis that if you put the right people on the job, the job will get done without the boss's help. Of course, if this were true a lot of managers could be eliminated, and organisations could rely on good recruiters.

Instead, he talks about the idea of preventative management in the same way you might talk about preventative maintenance for a machine or a car. Their definition is...

"Preventative management is the intervention of manipulating elements in a specific work environment to bring about a predicted outcome that would not have happened without that intervention."

Preventative management is about keeping things running well by doing things that deny people the opportunity to fail due to one or more of the 16 reasons for non-performance.

Below are the 16 reasons, according to Fournies and his colleagues:

1. They don't know why they should do it; they don't seem to care because they don't know why they should.
2. They don't know how to do it. Telling is not teaching and assuming they know costs you money.
3. They don't know what they are supposed to do. Strange but true, we pay them to do a lot of guessing.

4. They think your way will not work. Getting people to change is a big problem, and you need to sell them rather than tell them.
5. They think their way is better. Even smart people sometimes think the wrong things.
6. They think something else is more important. Working on the wrong things is expensive.
7. There is no positive consequence to them for doing it. People are moved by rewards, but managers don't use them enough.
8. They think they are doing it. After they've done it wrong, it's too late to tell them.
9. They are rewarded for not doing it. Managers often do this and yet don't know they are doing it.
10. They are punished for doing what they are supposed to do. Managers don't mean to do this, but it can result from the way they set things up.
11. They anticipate a negative consequence for doing it. Fearful employees don't perform well.
12. There is no negative consequence to them for poor performance. Managers often don't take corrective action.
13. Obstacles beyond their control: ignoring obstacles will not make them go away.
14. Their personal limits prevent them from performing. Managers are often confused about people's limitations.
15. Personal problems – everyone has personal problems that affect performance.
16. No one could do it. This is due to a manager's misunderstanding of the work situation.

Fournies book has a chapter on each of the 16 reasons and discusses the problem and a preventative solution for each one. I would recommend this as a useful text for any manager seeking to become an effective capability manager.

When the managers are on board with the idea that they need to manage capability, then you are well on the way to developing a new style of management that leads to a performance culture.

W. Edwards Deming quite aptly said...

"To successfully respond to the myriad of changes that shake the world, transformation into a new style of management is required."

Conclusion

Towards a performance culture

The most basic form of human stupidity is forgetting what we are trying to accomplish.

Friedrich Nietzsche

Culture is the learned assumptions on which people base their daily behaviour, '...the way we do things around here'. Culture drives the organisation, its actions and results. It guides how employees think, act and feel. It is the 'operating system' of the company, the organisational DNA.

There are many approaches, and many books and articles on culture and the art of changing it. And make no mistake; it is an art. Sometimes culture can be very stubborn and resist attempts to change it, and at other times it can change quite quickly in response to external stimuli. The art is knowing how to interact with the culture or make interventions that move the culture in the desired direction. The reason it is an art is that the things that drive a culture, such as values, beliefs and stories, are invisible. All that is visible is the impact these cultural drivers have on the people within the culture.

Do you remember learning about magnetism in school? A common and simple experiment involved sprinkling some iron filings on a piece of paper and then moving a magnet underneath the paper so you could see how the iron filings moved and followed the lines of the magnetic field. Culture is similar in that you can see the way it drives people's behaviour within the 'magnetic field' of the culture, but you cannot see the actual cultural drivers directly.

Once you understand how the magnetic field works, you can move the magnet in such a way that the iron filings line up where you want them. Now just imagine what would happen if there were two, or three, or even more magnets underneath your piece of paper. This is the case with organisational cultures where there are many competing forces that drive the culture from different directions. In effect, it is in a state of equilibrium between all these competing forces. Knowing which of the cultural forces to change and by how much, is the art of cultural change.

Here I am only concerned with how a focus on capability management can be part of a wider programme that is designed to change an organisational culture into one where good performance is 'the way we do things around here'.

Good performance happens when employees are doing what they are asked to do when they are asked to do it, and doing it sufficiently well so that the results they achieve deliver on the corporate strategy. Capability begets performance, so it is clear that a performance culture can only exist when there is a focus on ensuring that employees are capable at the point of work. In addition, in a performance culture there may well be a focus on other things, such as setting clear expectations, defining employees' roles, creating a trusting environment, and encouraging employees' growth and development.

In a performance culture, everyone understands that capability, as we have defined it in this book, is the key to performance. They understand that this is a causal relationship, and can see how there is a direct line of sight from capability at the point of work via performance to the organisational vision and mission.

In a performance culture, everyone becomes a performance consultant in that they understand the performance consultancy process, and whenever there is a performance problem, they automatically start looking for barriers to capability.

In a performance culture, everyone understands what capability is, and the fact that it is made up of different components that all need to be present in order for an employee to be capable at the point of work.

In a performance culture, the leaders and managers understand the concept of capability, and their behaviour shows that they have this understanding. They walk their talk. They fully support the performance consultancy process and insist that it is a fundamental way for people to approach business and performance problems.

In a performance culture, managers get fully involved with ensuring that the learning from any training course gets transferred back into their work area, because they have been personally involved in the performance consultancy process that decided that a training course was the best solution. They know which aspects of capability the training course can help, and which ones it can't.

In a performance culture, employees proactively look for ways to improve the processes they are working with and there is an atmosphere of constant incremental improvement.

As W. Edwards Deming pointed out...

> "Learning is not compulsory; it's voluntary. Improvement is not compulsory; it's voluntary. But to survive, we must learn."

So L&D has arrived at a fork in the road.

Down one fork, L&D will continue to be seen as order takers by the business and will continue to take orders from the business for training, or coaching, or e-learning, or other off-the-shelf learning services.

Down the other fork they will step onto the road less travelled and become a partner of the business because they become skilled performance consultants, and their input to achieving a high performing organisation is greatly valued.

Have you acknowledged the fork in the road yet?

Can you see that you have a choice?

Which road will you take?

As M. Scott Peck[66] said in *The Road Less Travelled...*

> "The truth is that our finest moments are most likely to occur when we are feeling deeply uncomfortable, unhappy, or unfulfilled. For it is only in such moments, propelled by our discomfort, that we are likely to step out of our ruts and start searching for different ways or truer answers."

As a performance consultant, you too have superpowers. You too have a billowing superhero cape and shiny underpants. For the good of the people around you, exercise your powers. And by the way, if you want to look good doing it, polish your underpants so they shine brightly in the sun.

My best wishes,

Paul Matthews

P.S. You are welcome to drop me a line if you have any comments or suggestions. My email address is paul.matthews@peoplealchemy.com

www.peoplealchemy.com

About the author

Paul's life and work history can only be described as a little unusual.

He grew up on a hill country farm in New Zealand and went on to study both Agriculture and Engineering at University. He graduated with first class honours and a couple of years later won a national farm machinery award for the design of a seed drill. The drills were exported by his employer to over 20 countries around the world. Years later, when he was travelling in Ecuador, he was amazed to see one of his seed drills up for sale in a second-hand farm machinery yard by the side of the road.

As many Kiwis do, he set off to see the world and travelled extensively, stopping along the way to earn money for the next adventure. He then landed what was to him a dream job, working for an adventure travel company leading overland expeditions into many remote areas of the world. All this experience, which lasted over four years, has given him some great stories to tell of far-flung places, from the Congo jungle to the Taklamakan desert in Western China. By the way, locals say the name means 'go in and you will never come out'.

Paul then 'got a real job' as an engineer in the UK. It proved quite a challenge to make the transition from travelling the wild places on the planet and needing to build a campfire each night, to working regular hours and commuting.

After some success, he was headhunted into a NASDAQ-quoted multi-national technology company, where he eventually held the role of Customer Services Director. It was during this time that he really started to appreciate the importance of learning, and was surprised that his adventures and the experience of observing people learn to cope with unfamiliar situations were so valuable in understanding learning. His curiosity led him into studying psychology and many other areas relating to how the mind works – knowledge which he could then translate back into the workplace.

The constraints of corporate life lost their appeal and Paul started his own company, People Alchemy Ltd, in 1999, working as a consultant, trainer and coach in the areas of management and leadership. Most of his clients were blue chip organisations and one client programme had over 1,200 delegates.

He soon recognised the need for more direct performance support and the importance of informal learning in all its guises, rather than the common L&D reliance on classroom training. Paul has a way of engaging people with this changing paradigm so they can grasp it, incorporating it into their own organisational learning and capability strategies. His approach helps people to fully cater to the learning needs of their staff so they can get the job done.

Informal Learning at Work

In January 2013 Paul published his book on *Informal Learning at Work: How To Boost Performance In Tough Times*.

Somewhat prophetically, the last line of his first book was 'Ultimately it is about capability'. He had no intention of writing a second book to expand on his ideas, but it happened because there was clearly a lot more to say.

In many ways the two books are companion volumes because so much of what is involved in enabling capability at the point of work needs to come from informal learning.

Informal learning is the powerhouse of learning in the workplace, and yet in many ways it is fragile. How can you manage informal learning without destroying the informality; and without destroying the very thing that makes it so powerful?

Studies have consistently shown that 70 per cent or more of the knowledge any person uses to do their job is learned informally. It is such a large part of how people get results at work that we need to be paying far more attention to it, and not throwing all our budget at traditional formal learning approaches.

So we need answers to questions like:

- How does it work?
- How do you manage it?
- How do you encourage it?
- How do you measure it?

- What role does Learning and Development play?
- Who else is doing it, and what is their experience?
- How do you use it in conjunction with formal learning?

In the book, you will discover how the role of anybody involved in workplace learning, enhancing capability and improving performance MUST change to successfully manage the critical shift in the way organisations need to cater to the learning needs of their employees. Deliberately harnessing the power of informal learning is the new way to tangibly improve worker capability and performance, right at the point of work.

This book shows you how, using practical advice from workplace learning experts, and examples and case studies from around the world.

Here are the chapter headings:

Chapter 1 – Survive and thrive with informal learning
Chapter 2 – The agile learning organisation
Chapter 3 – What is informal learning?
Chapter 4 – Informal learning in practice
Chapter 5 – The new L&D role
Chapter 6 – Practical things for you to do
Chapter 7 – More tools and ideas you can use
Chapter 8 – Managing your learnscape
Chapter 9 – Obstacles you may face
Chapter 10 – Getting managers more involved
Chapter 11 – Evaluating informal learning

It is clear that the role of learning and development is changing. This is both a challenge and an opportunity for L&D practitioners. Paul's book on informal learning at work gives you another way to seize the opportunity and make a difference in your organisation.

Here are some comments about *Informal Learning at Work*

"I smiled my way through Paul Matthews' book and I very much hope it will have more impact than my previous offerings. The continued underutilisation of work-based learning is short-sighted and wasteful. Informal learning

opportunities are not only plentiful, they are relatively inexpensive and always timely and relevant. I say a loud hurray to Paul Matthews' book. We all need it"
Peter Honey (Occupational psychologist and learning guru)

"Hurrah!! Finally, a book that doesn't just theorise about informal learning, but actually provides real-world, practical advice for making it happen."
Nicki Talbot (Director – L&D)

"A practical, inspirational guide to introducing informal learning into your organisation."
Christina Bush (L&D Manager)

"This is the new role for L&D – a paradigm shift for traditionalists."
Carol Bolton (OD Manager)

"This book has changed my mind-set and provided a framework and direction for how better performance can be achieved."
Adrian Kingswell (Head of L&D)

"Paul sets out his case succinctly and manages to distil, in a very easy to read book, clarity, common sense and a way forward from the often over-crowded debate on the future direction of workplace learning."
Derek Brimley (Learning Manager)

References

1 Wise, Gary, http://livinginlearning.com/
2 Gery, Gloria J. *Electronic Performance Support Systems: How and why to remake the workplace through the strategic application of technology.* Cambridge, MA: Ziff Institute, 1991
3 Senge, Peter M., *The Fifth Discipline: The Art and Practice of the Learning Organization,* Doubleday, 1990
4 'Breakthrough Performance in the New Work Environment: Identifying and Enabling the New High Performer', Corporate Executive Board, 2012
5 'State of the Global Workplace: Employee Engagement Insights for Business Leaders Worldwide 2013', Gallup Inc., 2013
6 Handcock, Thomas and Howlett, Warren, 'Transforming the L&D function for the New Work Environment', *Learning Quarterly* (Third Quarter 2013), the Corporate Executive Board, http://www.executiveboard.com
7 'Leadership and Management in the UK: The Key to Sustainable Growth', the UK Commission for Employment and Skills (UKCES), Crown, July 2012
8 'Big challenge brings big rewards: the big picture narrative', The UK Commission for Employment and Skills, March 2012
9 Woods, David, 'Poor management and leadership hold back UK's economic growth', *HR Magazine* (12 July 2012), http://www.hrmagazine.co.uk
10 'The New Learning Agenda – Talent, Technology and Change', case study by Towards Maturity
11 Harrison, Nigel, *Improving Employee Performance* Kogan Page, 2000
12 Arthur Jr., Winfred, Bennett Jr., Winston, Edens, Pamela S., and Bell, Suzanne T., 'Effectiveness of Training in Organisations – A Meta-Analysis of Design and Evaluation Features'

13 Woodfield, Kandy http://pushingattheedges.wordpress.com/2014/05/18/one-small-step-for-ld-one-big-step-for-workplace-learning/

14 Buckingham, Marcus, and Coffman, Curt, *First Break All the Rules: What the World's Greatest Managers Do Differently*, Pocket Books, 2005

15 Weber ,Emma, *Turning Learning Into Action: A proven methodology for effective transfer of learning*, Kogan Page, 2014

16 Dearborn, Jenny, 'The Pivotal Role Of The Learning Professional Today And Tomorrow', http://blogs.sap.com/innovation/human-resources/pivotal-role-learning-professional-today-tomorrow-01252393

17 Brache, Alan P., *How Organizations Work: Taking a Holistic Approach to Enterprise Health*, John Wiley & Sons, 2002

18 Webster, Susan, 'Bridging the Information Worker Productivity Gap: New Challenges and Opportunities for IT', (Sponsored by Adobe), IDC, September 2012

19 Harburg, Fred 'They're Buying Holes, Not Shovels' Chief Learning Officer, 2014, http://www.clomedia.com/articles/they_re_buying_holes_not_shovels

20 Harrison, Nigel, *How to be a True Business Partner by Performance Consulting*, Performance Consulting UK Ltd, 2008

21 Rummler, Geary A., and Brache, Alan P., *Improving Performance: How to Manage the White Space on the Organization Chart*, Jossey-Bass, Kindle Edition, 2012

22 O'Connor, Joseph, and McDermott, Ian, *The art of systems thinking: Essential Skills for Creativity and Problem Solving*, Thorsons, 1997

23 'Your Body's Systems', Pearson Education, 2007, http://www.factmonster.com/ipka/A0774536.html

24 Colbin, Annemarie, Ph.D., 'Systems Theory: An Overview', 2009, http://www.foodandhealing.com/research/systems_theory.htm

25 Rummler, Geary A., *Serious Performance Consulting According to Rummler*, International Society for Performance Improvement, John Wiley & Sons, 2007

26 Rummler, Geary A., and Brache, Alan P., *Improving Performance: How to Manage the White Space on the Organization Chart*, Jossey-Bass, Kindle Edition, 2012

27 Ordóñez, Lisa D., Schweitzer, Maurice E., Galinsky Adam D., Bazerman, Max H., 'Goals Gone Wild: The Systematic Side Effects of Overprescribing Goal Setting', *Academy of Management Perspectives*, Harvard Business School, 2009, http://www.hbs.edu/faculty/Publication%20Files/09-083.pdf

28 Rozwell, Carol, 'Do what I say, not what I do', Gartner Group, 2009, http://blogs.gartner.com/carol_rozwell/2009/11/18/do-what-i-say-not-what-i-do/

29 Quinn, Clark N., *Revolutionize Learning & Development: Performance And Innovation Strategy For The Information Age,* Wiley, 2014

30 Rummler, Geary A., and Brache, Alan P., *Improving Performance: How to Manage the White Space on the Organization Chart*, Jossey-Bass, Kindle Edition, 2012

31 Bird, Tom, and Cassell, Jeremy, *FT Guide to Business Training*, Financial Times Service, 2013

32 Smith, Rita, 'Aligning Learning With Business Strategy', November 2008, T+D, Vol. 62 Issue 11, p40

33 Hird, Martin, and Sparrow, Paul, 'Learning & Development: Seeking A Renewed Focus?', Lancaster University Management School, White Paper 12/01, October 2012

34 Meisinger, Susan R., 'Is Business a Foreign Language for HR?', *Human Resource Executive Online*, LRP Publications, 9 August 2010), http://www.hreonline.com/HRE/view/story.jhtml?id=495285666

35 Rothwell, William J., Lindholm, John E., and Wallick, William G., *What CEOs Expect from Corporate Training*, Amacom, 2003

36 'The LPI Capability Map: Six Month Report, June 2013', (The Learning and Performance Institute, 2013) http://www.learningandperformanceinstitute.com/capabilitymap.htm

37 Silber, Kenneth H. and Kearny, Lynn, *Organizational Intelligence: A Guide to Understanding the Business of Your Organization for HR, Training and Performance Consulting*, Pfeiffer, 2009

38 Bingham, Tony and Jeary, Tony, *Presenting Learning: Ensure CEOs get the Value of Learning*, American Society for Training & Development, 2007

39 Mundy, J. Craig, 'Why HR Still Isn't a Strategic Partner' *HBR Blog Network,* Harvard Business Review, 7 May 2012, http://blogs.hbr.org/2012/07/why-hr-still-isnt-a-strategic-partner/

40 'Rethinking Human Resources in a Changing World'. Study undertaken for KPMG by the Economist Intelligence Unit, September 2012

41 'What is Working Class?', *BBC Magazine*, 25 January 2007, http://news.bbc.co.uk/2/hi/uk_news/magazine/6295743.stm

42 National Readership Survey, http://www.nrs.co.uk/

43 Ebbinghaus, Herman, *Memory: A Contribution to Experimental Psychology. Classics in the History of Psychology*. Tr. by Henry A Ruger, and Bussenius Clara E., Teachers College, Columbia University 1913, http://psychclassics.yorku.ca/Ebbinghaus/

44 Adams, Linda, 'Learning a New Skill is Easier Said Than Done', *Gordon Training Institute*, http://www.gordontraining.com/free-workplace-articles/learning-a-new-skill-is-easier-said-than-done/

45 Rosenberg, Marc J., 'At the Moment of Need: The Case for Performance Support', The ELearning Guild, June 2013

46 Wise, Gary, 'Feeding the Performance Zone with EPS', May 2014, http://livinginlearning.com/2014/05/01/feeding-the-performance-zone-with-eps/

47 Sparrow, Betsy et al, 'Google Effects on Memory: Cognitive Consequences of Having Information at Our Fingertips', July 2011

48 Williams, David K., 'How Much Do Bad Bosses Cost American Businesses?' Forbes Magazine, 24 September 2012,http://www.forbes.com/sites/davidkwilliams/2012/09/24/how-much-do-bad-bosses-cost-american-businesses/

49 Peacock, Louisa 'Bad management "costs UK £19bn a year"', The Telegraph, 10 November 2011, http://www.telegraph.co.uk/finance/jobs/hr-news/8879895/Bad-management-costs-UK-19bn-a-year.html/

50 Weinberg, Gerald M., The Secrets of Consulting: A Guide to Giving and Getting Advice Successfully, Dorset House Publishing, April 1985

51 Stone, Ron Drew, Aligning Training for Results: A Process and Tools That Link Training to Business, Pfeiffer, November 2008

52 Wise, Gary, 'Finding the Learning & Performance Black Box', April 2014, http://livinginlearning.com/2014/04/07/finding-the-learning-performance-black-box/

53 Taylor, Donald H., 'Are you in the Training Ghetto?', April 2013, http://donaldhtaylor.wordpress.com/2013/04/15/are-you-in-the-training-ghetto/

54 Harrison, Nigel How to Deal with Power and Manipulation, Performance Consulting, 2014

55 Davis, Barbara, Tools for Teaching, John Wiley & Sons, February 2009

56 Kirkpatrick, James D., and Kirkpatrick, Wendy Kayser, Kirkpatrick Then and Now: A Strong Foundation For The Future, CreateSpace Independent Publishing Platform, September 2009

57 Gottfredson, Conrad, Ph.D., and Mosher, Bob, Innovative Performance Support: Strategies and Practices for Learning in the Workflow, McGraw Hill, 2011

58 Lazear, Edward, Shaw, Kathryn, and Stanton, Christopher, 'The Value of Bosses', Stanford University, September 2011

59 'Improving Talent Management Outcomes', Corporate Leadership Council Corporate Executive Board, 2007

60 Beck, Randall, and Harter, James, 'Why Good Managers Are So Rare', Harvard Business Review, March 2014, http://blogs.hbr.org/2014/03/why-good-managers-are-so-rare/

61 Manzoni, Jean-François, and Barsoux, Jean-Louis, 'The Set-Up-To-Fail Syndrome', *Harvard Business Review,* March 2014, http://hbr.org/1998/03/the-set-up-to-fail-syndrome/ar/1

62 Armstrong, Michael, *How to be an Even Better Manager: A Complete A-Z of Proven Techniques and Essential Skills,* 6th Edition, Kogan Page, 2004

63 'Real-life leaders: closing the knowing-doing gap', CIPD, September 2013, https://www.cipd.co.uk/hr-resources/research/real-life-leaders.aspx

64 Blanchard, Ken, and Johnson, Spencer, *The One Minute Manager*, Fontana, 1983

65 Fournies, Ferdinand F., *Why Employees Don't Do What They're Supposed To and What You Can Do About It*, McGraw Hill, 1999

66 Peck, M. Scott, *The Road Less Travelled*, Arrow, 1990

Index

M

workforce, percentage of blue collar
    workers, 63
workplace
    culture, 83, 151-2
    modifications, 75
World Economic Forum report: *Global Competitiveness*, 12

Z

Ziglar, Z., 70